...YERS LOSE THEIR WAY

JEAN STEFANCIC AND RICHARD DELGADO

How Lawyers Lose Their Way

A PROFESSION FAILS ITS CREATIVE MINDS

Duke University Press   Durham and London   2005

© 2005 Duke University Press

All rights reserved

Printed in the United States of America

on acid-free paper ∞

Designed by CH Westmoreland

Typeset in Bembo

by Keystone Typesetting, Inc.

LIBRARY OF CONGRESS

CATALOGING-IN-PUBLICATION DATA

Stefancic, Jean.

How lawyers lose their way :

a profession fails its creative minds

/ Jean Stefancic, Richard Delgado.

p. cm.

Includes bibliographical references and index.

ISBN 0-8223-3454-2 (cloth : alk. paper)

ISBN 0-8223-3563-8 (pbk. : alk. paper)

1. Practice of law—United States—

Psychological aspects. 2. Lawyers—job

satisfaction—United States.

I. Delgado, Richard. II. Title.

KF300.S698 2005   340'.023'73—dc22

2004015808

Invent the age, invent the metaphor.

Without a credible structure of law

a society is inconceivable.

Without a workable poetry no society

can conceive a man.

—Archibald MacLeish,

Apologia (1972)

Contents

Acknowledgments

We drafted major portions of this book at three residential centers: the Liguria Study Center for the Arts and Humanities of the Bogliasco Foundation in Bogliasco, Italy; the Centrum Creative Residency Program in Port Townsend, Washington; and the Center for Social Justice of the University of California School of Law in Berkeley. In Italy we gratefully acknowledge the support and inspiration of the center's staff, particularly Anna Maria Quaiat, Ivana Folle, and Alan Rowlin, and of Professor Massimo Bacigalupo of the University of Genoa. The residential fellows David Young, Robert Hahn, Nicole Rafter, Janine Massard, Max Kosloff, and Joyce Kosloff made our stay lively and memorable. At Centrum, we thank Sally Rodgers and a supportive staff for enabling us to spend a month in exhilarating surroundings. Thanks as well to Mary Louise Frampton and the staff of the Center for Social Justice for a residency in fall 2003, which enabled us to complete the final stages of this book, and to Clark Smith, who encouraged us to write it in the first place.

The University of Colorado Law School, Dean Harold Bruff, and the University of Pittsburgh Law School, Dean David Herring, provided steadfast and generous support over several years. At Pittsburgh the Document Technology Center under the direction of LuAnn Driscoll prepared the manuscript with intelligence and dispatch. Two law students, Anna Fredericksen-Cherry and Andrea Wang, now members of the bar, read the manuscript and provided feedback and suggestions on sections dealing with legal education. Jillian Lloyd and Marla Kerr researched sections concerning two professions.

We benefited greatly as well from the support and assistance of the Library of Congress, Manuscript Division, and the Beinecke Library at Yale for giving us access to unpublished material from their Pound and MacLeish collections.

In Italy, the Biblioteca Internazionale, Città di Rapallo: International

Library and Reading Rooms, Villa Tigullio, opened its collection of Ezra Pound materials to us; we thank their generous, bilingual staff. Finally, at the University of Colorado we benefited greatly from the talents of Jane Thompson, faculty services librarian, and her assistant Manuel Santos, who seemed able to get us any materials we needed in no time flat, and at the University of California, from the ebullient and expert services of Michael Levy.

We gave faculty workshops on aspects of this book at the law schools of the University of California, Davis, the University of Wisconsin, the University of Florida, the University of San Diego, the University of Missouri, Kansas City, the University of California, Berkeley, Quinnipiac University, Cleveland State University, the University of Nevada, Las Vegas, and the University of Pittsburgh, and acknowledge the many suggestions and contributions of the participants. Small portions of this book appeared earlier in the Southern California and Michigan law reviews, whose editors assisted greatly in their preparation.

Introduction

WHY ARE LAWYERS SO UNHAPPY?

This book names and confronts an overabundance of formalism, which was first identified in the law but now appears almost everywhere. Formalism is a habit of mind and a type of social organization that attempts perversely to narrow one's focus beyond that which a situation requires to render justice to it. The ideational analogue of the crass industrialization that D. H. Lawrence deplored, formalism—the regimentation of thought and reasoning—operates in a similar fashion, taking the life out of work and the professions, depriving them of juice, richness, concreteness, and anything else that might render them of human interest. If taken to extremes, it can mean the death of inquiry, the atrophy of cultural diversity, and a loss of opportunities for intellectual and disciplinary cross-fertilization.

In law, formalism is connected to the rule of precedent and conservative judging. In legal education, formalism manifests itself in the teaching of rules and doctrines at the expense of social implications and policy. It exalts internal values such as consistency over ambiguity, rationality over emotion, rules over social context or competing interests and narratives. In literature, it appears as the pinched desire to restrict study to the traditional western canon. In literary interpretation, it focuses attention on the text and its meaning, rather than on the author or the setting in which it was written. In history, it limits inquiry to wars and great men and excludes the stories of immigrants, women, and laborers. In public policy debates, it is associated with the anti-immigrant impulse and the desire to keep the nation demographically pure.

Formalism is satisfied with, does not even question, narrowly defined views of life and knowledge. It eliminates the intellectual independence of feisty lawyers, questioning doctors, and critical scholars who wish to think outside disciplinary boxes. It tries to make into a machine that which cannot be a machine—a person. Harmful for society and deadening to the soul, formalism sets us up for cooptation by bureaucracies, large corporations, and the state. More often than not, we do not know when and how this happens.

This book begins by recounting a single, arresting example of a good mind who confronted formalism and suffered as a result. In part I, we tell the story of the unexamined relationship between two eminent literary figures, Ezra Pound and Archibald MacLeish. Pound, this country's foremost modernist poet and one of the most innovative in the twentieth century anywhere, was manic and given to excess. A womanizer and social provocateur, he nevertheless befriended many young writers, both in the United States and abroad, earning a devoted discipleship. In midlife, while living in Rapallo, Italy, he embraced bizarre economic theories and became an admirer of Mussolini and Italian fascism, on behalf of which he made a series of wartime propaganda broadcasts.

MacLeish was Ezra Pound's direct opposite. Well-bred and educated at elite schools, he practiced law during his early years, but maintained a lifelong fascination with poetry. Indeed, while pursuing a career in law and journalism, he published a number of collections of poetry and verse plays, and toward the end of his career was appointed to a chair of rhetoric at Harvard. In between he held high positions in government and the Eastern establishment. He was a statesman's statesman, avoiding scandal at all costs.

As the reader will see, MacLeish, a young blue-blood lawyer writing poetry in his spare time and toying with the idea of a literary career, sought out Pound for advice. Pound counseled MacLeish about his writing, sometimes mercilessly. After an arduous period spent trying to develop his talent in Paris in the 1920s, MacLeish returned to the States where he became a writer for *Fortune* magazine and pursued a career in government service during the Roosevelt era. Yet, despite the outward appearance of happiness, MacLeish was unfulfilled, always wondering what he might have been had he pursued his other calling wholeheartedly. Years later, MacLeish came to Pound's rescue after Pound had been incarcerated for ten years at St. Elizabeths Hospital for the Criminally Insane in lieu of a treason trial. Working with others, he arranged that Pound be retried and acquitted with the understanding that he would soon leave the United States for his beloved Italy. As it turned out, just as MacLeish earlier needed the anarchic spirit of Pound, Pound later benefited from the orderly elegance of the lawyer MacLeish.

From this extraordinary relationship, we draw lessons about the plight of dissatisfied lawyers, and perhaps other professionals, trapped in worlds that give them power, prestige, and affluence, but not personal satisfaction, much less creative fulfillment. Building on both personality theory and contemporary critical thought, we show how the story of our country's most eminent lawyer-statesman-poet and its most brilliant imagist poet exposes tensions that modern civilization produces, but to which it has yet to find a solution. With the increasing turn to technology and the routinization, specialization, and narrowness of many professional lives, the urgency of these problems can only increase.

In part II, we show that the problems MacLeish struggled with as a young lawyer have not abated. Even though progressive movements in the law, such as critical legal studies, feminism, and critical race theory have made inroads, making law more humane and broad-gauged, many lawyers today are miserable, and for many of the same reasons that haunted MacLeish. Separate chapters summarize the professional discontents of contemporary lawyers—the high rates of dropout, burnout, alcohol and drug addiction, divorce, and suicide that many of these high-paid professionals display. This dissatisfaction begins, for many, with law school, and the demands of legal practice—billable hours, narrow specialization, and the pressures of achieving partnership—simply amplify that discontent. Lawyers' unhappiness with their own work lives finds a counterpart in the public's disenchantment with lawyers, whom their clients are apt to see as driven, self-absorbed individuals who do not return phone calls and like nothing better than to fight and drive up the cost of any legal transaction.

Drawing on the story of Archibald MacLeish and Ezra Pound, we show that lawyers' unhappiness contains both a conceptual dimension, concerned with how they theorize what they do, and a phenomenological one that embraces the felt experiences of law and lawyering. But the misery, as well as the habit of mind that seeks regularity, routine, orderliness, and formulaic resolution of problems are not limited to law. In particular, chapter 6 illustrates how many of the miseries that bedevil physicians stem from many of the same sources that plague lawyers.

Need we say it? We are interested in broad systemic forces that plague lawyers because of the nature of their work—that are, in short, inherent in lawyering and, perhaps, other forms of work. Just as unhappy families can be unhappy in infinitely many ways, so can lawyers: this one because he hates his managing partner, that one because he dislikes his commute, another one because her husband does not understand her. We are interested in structural forces that impinge on the lives of all lawyers, making their work narrower, less creative, and more pressured than it needs to be.

Human minds and spirits are not machines. They rebel, knowing that something is wrong when given work to do, and ways to think about it, that assure failure and eliminate much that is most interesting, vital, and unique. Although our story is mainly about lawyers, it carries implications for all of society. Just as we need feisty, thoughtful, independent lawyers as a counterweight to excessive statism and overbearing corporations, we need caring physicians, happy in their work, who are able to place their patients' well-being above paperwork and managed care. We need teachers who do not teach to standardized tests, and university administrators willing to back curricular experiments without worrying constantly about accountability.

The final pages of the book enlist cultural history to sketch how our predicament began and suggest a few means by which we might counter it. If, as we suspect, the habit of mind that is formalism is like a self-replicating virus, endlessly seeking new hosts, the human spirit will eventually suffer irreparable harm. We write this book with the hope of helping to ward off that result.

HOW LAWYERS LOSE THEIR WAY

Ezra Pound
(November 1963). *Photo by David Lees. Reprinted with permission of Time Life Pictures / Getty Images.*

Archibald MacLeish.
Photo by Verner Reed. Reprinted with permission of Time Life Pictures / Getty Images.

1 Panthers and Pinstripes

But what, then, is the business of poetry? Precisely to make sense of the chaos of our lives. To create the understanding of our lives. To compose an order which the bewildered, angry heart can recognize. To imagine a man.
—Archibald MacLeish, *Apologia* (1972)

But in the caged panther's eyes: Nothing.
Nothing that you can do.
—Ezra Pound, *The Pisan Cantos*, Canto 83 (1948)

Archibald MacLeish and Ezra Pound were extraordinary figures: Mac-Leish his country's most noted lawyer-poet-public servant, Pound its greatest modernist poet.[1] Their relationship was just as extraordinary, al-though until the recent publication of MacLeish's letters and oral history and of his son's memoirs, and the unsealing of Pound's legal files, its story could not be told.[2] Now it can be, by piecing together letter and reply (often from separate sources) over forty years, as we have done for the first time. Pound, manic and given to excess, became seriously unbalanced in his middle years, expounding racist and anti-Semitic views, taunting Mac-Leish and other American loyalists during the Second World War, and broadcasting on behalf of the fascist regime in Italy. His case stands vir-tually alone in the annals of American literature. No American writer before had been indicted for treason, declared insane, and committed to a mental hospital for an indeterminate time.[3]

MacLeish had little in common with Pound. Refined, and educated at the best schools, he rose easily to prominence in the country's literary and political establishments. Yet after an earlier spurning at Pound's hands,

MacLeish was instrumental in bringing about the poet's release from a mental hospital in 1958, acting discreetly behind the scenes and taking little credit for it. Conventional explanations of MacLeish's role rest either on sympathy—MacLeish felt sorry for the great poet—or on public calling—MacLeish intervened because Pound's predicament was becoming an embarrassment for the United States.

Understanding MacLeish's role in the Pound affair requires a deeper exploration of his character and his place in American law and public life. After recounting the salient facts of the Pound affair, particularly the points at which MacLeish's career intersected with Pound's, we offer interpretive explanations of MacLeish's role, one based on MacLeish's divided personality as a lawyer-writer, another based on changes in the position of the United States in world politics and MacLeish's role in ushering in those changes. Finally, we offer a third explanation, one which cuts across the other two, based on shifting understandings of legal thought and education.

We find in the story of Pound and MacLeish elements of a morality tale. MacLeish was an excellent legal technician who from the beginning hungered for something else. Trained in the humanities but caught up in an arid legal world, he struggled to integrate the two sides of his personality. But in spite of his prodigious talent, MacLeish's panther remained caged for most of his life.[4]

1 The Caged Panther

EZRA POUND

It was a fine spring day in Cambridge, Massachusetts, but inside the dark-paneled study of the famous professor the scene approached bedlam. The goateed, red-maned visitor, a distinguished poet and émigré who had returned to the United States to receive an honorary degree from his alma mater, was entertaining a rapt but skeptical audience of Harvard faculty. Waving his arms, his voice rising and falling, he was holding forth on far-fetched economic and racial theories many removes from his field of competence. A few of the listeners looked intrigued; several contemptuous. They shot question after question at the visitor, hoping to catch him off guard. Undeterred, he pressed on, his countenance taking on the aspect of a madman.

Partway through the proceedings, a tall, distinguished-looking gentleman with a patrician brow shook his head, muttered something under his breath, and stalked out.

Though Ezra Pound was born in Idaho in 1885, his family moved east when he was two years old, settling in Philadelphia, where his father took a position as assayer at the U.S. Mint.[1] Later, Pound vividly recalled seeing his father weigh a man's signature written in gold and watching workers shovel gold coins into counting machines.[2] The only child of parents with aristocratic pretensions—his paternal grandfather had been a lieutenant governor and U.S. congressman from Wisconsin, while his mother was related to the poet Longfellow—Pound readily absorbed the prejudices of his family and their middle-class friends.[3] Writing of his boyhood, he described waves of immigrants "sweeping along Eighth Avenue in the splendor of their vigorous unwashed animality."[4]

Pound enrolled at the University of Pennsylvania at fifteen, already knowing that he wanted to be a poet.[5] Unfortunately, he also went to great lengths to act like one, affecting flagrantly unconventional manners and dress. His indifferent academic performance, strange ways, and self-absorption put off his classmates, some of whom threw him into a campus pond.[6] An attempt at pledging a fraternity ended predictably in disaster.[7] Disappointed with his reception, Pound transferred to Hamilton College in his third year, graduated in 1905, and returned to Penn for his master's degree.[8] By that time he had taught himself eight languages and met William Carlos Williams and Hilda Doolittle (H.D.), both of whom became major American poets and remained his friends for life.[9]

A short-lived teaching career ended badly. Pound's unorthodox ideas, flamboyant appearance, and sexual adventuring scandalized the community at Wabash College in Crawfordsville, Indiana, and made it necessary for him to leave after a scant four months.[10] With financial support from his father, he sailed for Venice in 1908, then moved to England where he made his way into the bohemian literary scene of London.[11] There, in less than two years, Pound published four collections of poetry of such striking originality that continental reviewers heralded the arrival of a new genius.[12] Invited to lecture at London Polytechnic Institute, he also received an appointment as foreign correspondent for *Poetry* magazine.[13] At this time English and American poetry was full of sentimentality and moral didacticism. Pound set out to reform it.[14]

A return visit to the United States in 1910 brought nothing but disappointment. Pound's writing received mixed reviews and he could find little work.[15] Even an attempt to set up a business selling an anti-syphilitic drug proved a failure.[16] Returning to London the following year, he soon became a fixture at literary gatherings, often wearing sombreros, earrings, capes, masks, and other dramatic garb.[17] Young poets flocked to him, receiving encouragement, praise, and the advice to write simply and in their own voices.[18] He met and influenced a host of writers who went on to become major figures, including T. S. Eliot, Robert Frost, Rabindranath Tagore, and William Butler Yeats,[19] with whom he shared an interest in mysticism and the conviction that creativity was linked to sexual energy.[20]

Pound's persona at this time was unabashedly bohemian. He despised convention and when bored, for example at a dinner party, would eat the flowers of a table setting.[21] But when excited, he would lean forward and gesticulate so energetically that the chair on which he was sitting would strain or break.[22] A novelist who met Pound in London described him as a "tall, slight nervous young fellow, with the face of a scholarly satyr, and a pointed beard of the same [red] color," who "endangered every chair he sat on"[23] and devoured enormous quantities of food.[24] A reviewer in the *New Age* saw a "rebel against all conventions except sanity; there is something robustly impish about him. He writes with fresh beauty and vigour . . . revolting against a crepuscular spirit in modern poetry."[25]

Pound began translating Chinese and Japanese poetry when he agreed to edit the notebooks of Ernest Fenollosa, one of the first westerners to recognize and celebrate Asian literary traditions.[26] Among Pound's greatest achievements, according to MacLeish, may have been including Fenollosa's famous essay "The Chinese Written Character as a Medium for Poetry" in the back pages of his own *Instigations*, after a number of unsuccessful attempts to publish it in literary journals.[27] Pound became the acknowledged architect of modern poetry, dismantling the ornate language of the Victorian tradition and replacing it with sharp images, precise words, and metrical variation.[28] As one critic put it, "Perfection was what he was after, to convey 'an exact impression of exactly what one means in such a way as to exhilarate . . . Technique is the only gauge and test of a man's lasting sincerity.' "[29] His own objectives in writing he described as "1. To paint the thing as I see it. 2. Beauty. 3. Freedom from didacticism." And, 4. To build on the work of others.[30] "An image," he wrote, "is that which presents an intellectual and emotional complex in an instant in time."[31] His poem *In a Station of the Metro*, for example, uses a mere fourteen words to convey his impression of a Parisian subway platform:

> The apparition of these faces in a crowd;
> Petals on a wet, black bough.[32]

Or consider these lines, describing the loss of a loved one, translated from the Chinese poet Liu Ch'e':

> There is no sound of foot-fall, and the leaves
> Scurry into heaps and lie still,
> And she the rejoicer of the heart is beneath them:
> A wet leaf that clings to the threshold.[33]

Or these, satirizing the Middle English poem "Sumer is icumen in":

> Winter is icummen in,
> Lhude sing Goddamm,
> Raineth drop and staineth slop,
> And how the wind doth ramm!
>   Sing: Goddamm[34]

Pound wrote prodigiously, his output including reviews of literature, music, and art,[35] and his fame soon spread throughout the world, yet his income was barely enough for his needs and he was obliged to accept money from his family and patrons.[36] (At one point, he even considered selling his boots.)[37] This apparently did not much bother him, for when he had more than he needed, he gave it away to writers more needy than he.[38]

Devastated by the First World War, London ceased to be a hub of literary innovation. So Pound left for Paris, where he continued to write and support aspiring writers, artists, and musicians.[39] The city was familiar to him; he had been there regularly since before the war and had met a number of older French writers of the Symbolist school. Unlike many of the American émigrés who followed and did not immerse themselves in the culture or even learn the language, Pound did.[40] (Archibald MacLeish, who was to come later, did so as well.)[41]

Pound and Gertrude Stein became slightly antagonistic centers of literary ferment for the crowd of émigrés that was then gathering.[42] He gave freely of his advice and assistance. Believing that technique could be taught, he wrote forcefully and openly about his own creative process and his approach to writing.[43] As one critic put it, "For this reason, other men accepted him as their teacher, and men of strong, original talent—Yeats, Eliot, Joyce—were willing to listen to his instructions."[44] Those instructions included his famous exhortations: "It is better to present one Image in a lifetime than to produce voluminous works," "Use no superfluous word, no adjective which does not reveal something," and "Go in fear of abstractions."[45] He raised money for Eliot and edited *The Waste Land*.[46] He helped Hemingway to hone his clean prose style and befriended James Joyce, even sending him a pair of used but sturdy brown shoes.[47] His own work, consisting largely of a series of "Cantos," was highly original;[48] yet even that early work betrays a dark side, containing scattered disparagements of banks, usury, and Jews.[49] Earlier in London, Pound had met Clifford Douglas, a British engineer who had become intrigued by the way in which during peacetime, when capacity for production was high, ordinary citizens lacked enough money to purchase necessities. Yet in wartime, there seemed to be enough money for everything.[50] In his book *Economic Democracy* (1920),[51] which Pound reviewed favorably, Douglas argued that individuals should only be paid for labor that resulted in a product—goods, food, works of art.[52] But no one should be permitted to make money from money—that is, from rents, investments, interest, or dividends. This practice, which he called usury, was the source of most of England's ills because it allowed a small group to control the economy and money supply.[53]

Poor and acutely aware of the poverty of other artists, Pound fell under the influence of Douglas and his "social credit" theory.[54] Though not himself a fascist, Douglas had incorporated into his work ideas from *The Protocols of the Learned Elders of Zion*.[55] That anonymous book professed to expose a secret plan by which Jews would take over the world economy by gaining control of banking, the press, and business.[56] Biased since childhood against foreigners, blacks, and Jews, Pound's mind seized on Douglas's views; the crash of 1929 only confirmed them. Later, when he learned that Benito Mussolini had freed the Italian monetary system from international banking, his admiration knew no bounds.[57]

With their move to Italy in 1925, Pound and his wife Dorothy became even more isolated from American thought and his economic and political ideas increasingly extreme.[58] He also became more critical of the United States, especially the "passport nuisance" (because he traveled a great deal), U.S. copyright laws (because of the *Ulysses* affair), and article 211 of the U.S. Penal Code (because of its definition of obscenity).[59] He dabbled in strange educational theories,[60] just as earlier he had succumbed to crackpot notions such as vorticism,[61] and wrote the scenario for a movie praising fascism.[62] He also requested an audience with Mussolini in 1932, and after speaking briefly with him became a devoted follower.[63] His book *Jefferson and / or Mussolini*, rejected by forty publishers before its issue in 1935, argued that the two leaders were strikingly similar.[64] Its last line was: "Towards which I assert again my own firm belief that the Duce will stand not with despots and the lovers of power but with the lovers of ORDER."[65] Like

MacLeish, Pound was also a devoted follower and admirer of Jefferson.[66] Pound wrote hundreds of letters preaching monetary reform to newspapers, magazines, and public figures, including President Roosevelt, Albert Einstein, Huey Long, Father Charles Coughlin, and even the mystery writer Dorothy Sayers.[67] "I personally know of no social evil that cannot be cured, or very largely cured, economically," he wrote.[68] At one stage, Pound even attempted to combine the doctrines of Mussolini and Lenin in a grand synthesis of economic doctrine. He was not successful in persuading others of this pairing.[69] He may have been more successful in persuading them that "the effects of social [and economic] evil show first in the arts."[70]

Pound began employing dialect, odd punctuation, and peculiar abbreviations—eccentricities that when combined with his increasingly extreme political views made friends suspect that he had become unhinged.[71] Their concerns deepened when Pound returned to the United States in 1939 to promote his theories, accept an honorary degree from his alma mater, Hamilton College, and seek a position in the U.S. government.[72] Of course, no one took him seriously. He sought an interview with President Roosevelt, but was shunted off to Secretary of Agriculture Henry Wallace.[73] MacLeish, who met him during this time at a gathering at Harvard and was soon to praise him in the *Atlantic Monthly* as the first modern poet and a hater of rhetoric and overblown language,[74] was so distressed that he left the room.[75]

Stung a second time, Pound returned to Italy, where he recorded a series of vitriolic radio broadcasts—125 in all—extolling fascism and Mussolini's government.[76] Because Roosevelt had not reformed the banking system as Mussolini had, according to Pound, he was in league with the Jews, who were promoting the war effort for their own gain.[77] In one of these broadcasts, Pound accused Archibald MacLeish, who was then serving as director of the Office of Facts and Figures (the government propaganda office during the Second World War), of filing "a gangster's brief": "I [ask] Archie to say openly why he handed out four billion dollars in excess profits . . . between 1932 and 1940 . . . to a dirty gang of kikes and hyper-kikes on the London gold exchange firms. Why is that expected to help America? . . . Had you the sense to eliminate Roosevelt and his Jews . . . at the last election, you would not now be at war."[78]

Of course, MacLeish had done no such thing, though he had served as a writer for *Fortune* magazine during that period.[79] Despite Pound's tone of outraged betrayal, he and MacLeish had met face to face only once in recent years, during Pound's return visit to the United States in 1939, and perhaps briefly in Paris during MacLeish's period there.[80] They knew each other mainly through mutual friends and correspondence regarding Mac-Leish's poetry, which Pound had excoriated ("You understand I am putting on the heavy hammer; if I don't, the criticism is of no use, and we get off into mere conversation and politesse. . . . Am saying all the unpleasant things I can. Otherwise no use in writing.").[81]

Because of his Italian radio broadcasts, Pound was indicted in absentia in the District of Columbia for treason in July 1943.[82] After Mussolini fled in the face of the Allied advance, Pound continued broadcasting and writing in Italian newspapers. Italian partisans arrested him in May 1945 and transferred him to the U.S. military authorities in Pisa, where he was imprisoned in a reinforced steel "gorilla cage," on display by day and illuminated by spotlight at night.[83] He was returned to the United States in November 1945, a broken man.[84] At his preliminary arraignment, Pound told the judge that he wanted Archibald MacLeish to testify for him at his trial and that he had met him earlier, but to no avail.[85] He also insisted that he had never meant to hurt the American cause, but merely wanted to educate the American people.[86] A few months later, in a courthouse in Washington, after hearing testimony by four psychiatrists, a jury deliberated for only three minutes before finding Pound to be of unsound mind.[87] He was remanded to St. Elizabeths Hospital for the Criminally Insane until he could be restored to sanity.[88]

During his years of incarceration, Pound received a steady stream of visitors, including old friends, sycophants, racists, and members of the lunatic fringe.[89] He wrote *The Pisan Cantos*, based on his Italian confinement, which won the Bollingen Prize in 1949.[90] At first, there was little incentive to resolve his situation. His actions had incensed opinion makers and stirred public sentiment against him.[91] Yet at the same time, he lived well at government expense.[92] The chief psychiatrist at St. Elizabeths, Dr. Winfred Overholser, took pride and pleasure in his famous patient, seeing to it that he had everything he needed for his work.[93] The 1950s dragged on; McCarthyism came and went; but Pound was still impounded. There was little pressure to release him.

2 Pinstripes

Born in 1892, a few years after Pound, Archibald MacLeish grew up in Glencoe, Illinois, where his father, a Scottish émigré, managed a successful retail store and was a founder and trustee of the University of Chicago.[1] His mother, Martha Hilliard, a Mayflower descendent and welfare reformer, served as the first principal of a seminary for women.[2] MacLeish enjoyed a comfortable and secure childhood, enriched by his mother's readings from children's books, the Bible, Shakespeare, and Dante.[3] He attended the Hotchkiss School in Connecticut and later Yale.[4] By then, in his own words, he "was already writing perfectly dreadful verses, but writing a great many of them."[5]

Yale was then a school for gentlemen, clubby and not particularly distinguished in scholarship.[6] The small English department specialized in eighteenth-century writers and Victorians such as Tennyson and Browning, the very influences that Pound, a continent away, was beginning to attack. MacLeish wrote verse and won minor school prizes, but remained unsatisfied. Later he reflected, "I loved Yale deeply . . . but it wasn't an educational institution. It lacked the sort of thing that I felt at once when I went to the Harvard Law School and would occasionally cross over to the Yard."[7]

Yale also lacked a sense of noblesse oblige, or even of engagement. Indeed, for the thirty-fifth reunion of MacLeish's class, Clarence Mendell, a distinguished professor of classics at Yale, wrote, "Yours was the last class with whom I read Petronius and Euripides and Horace with a sense of permanence and security that made possible for us a leisurely sympathy with them, ignoring the storms and wreckage of the centuries and the continent that lay between."[8]

When MacLeish graduated, he had little clear idea of what he wanted to do. Writing beckoned, but he hesitated to make the sacrifices that the writer's life might require. He opted instead for law school, with the understanding that his father would increase his allowance after one year to permit him to marry his fiancée, Ada Hitchcock.[9] Although he entered law school as a compromise—it was better than going into business or teaching[10]—he unexpectedly found his studies engrossing: "The law school was an extraordinary intellectual experience and I discovered early that I was quite good at it. . . . [it] was a means to livelihood, but what I hadn't counted on was that it was a very exciting intellectual discipline."[11]

He also found it quite challenging. According to his son William: "Harvard shook the Yale stuffing out of Archibald MacLeish. He arrived full of honors and conceit and within days found himself pinned by far more experienced minds on the Socratic mats of the law school. That riled and excited him."[12] A little later, however, he changed his tune, writing to a former classmate from Yale: "[I] am completely swallowed by law. . . . It is a perfect jungle—the farther in you go the deeper the tangle gets and the more lies out behind you to be kept in mind. I won't say that it has not its fascination, for it has, but it also fills me with a very real rebellion."[13] He finished his first year with A grades,[14] yet wrote to his father: "Life is too short to do work which is as deadening as this. My two remaining free summers I intend to devote to the great mass of reading I have yet to do and for the doing of which my mind is so thirsty. Law and literature are, of course, incompatible, but I want to acquire a sufficient background so that if I am ever able to turn to the thing I most love I shall be able to undertake creative work at once."[15]

During his second year of law school, MacLeish continued to mourn his missed opportunity to write. His letters to his friend Francis Bangs describe meetings with minor poets and include poems that MacLeish had submitted unsuccessfully for publication.[16] When the United States entered the war in Europe in 1917, MacLeish knew at once that he must go.[17] Although entitled to a deferment, he enlisted in an ambulance unit, then transferred to the Yale field artillery unit, where he served until the end of the war.[18]

MacLeish then reenrolled at Harvard, graduated with honors, and passed the bar in the fall of 1919.[19] After exploring editorial work with literary and political magazines, he rejected both legal practice and editing for a temporary position teaching government at Harvard. He had already published a small collection of poetry while at the front and continued work on another.[20] One of his war poems had drawn an analogy between war and the law, anticipating his later development:

A Library of Law
Adjudicated quarrels of mankind,
Brown row on row!—how well these lawyers bind
Their records of dead sin,—as if they feared
The hate might spill and their long shelves besmeared
With slime of human souls—brown row on row
Span on Philistine span, a greasy show
Of lust and lies and cruelty, dried grime
Streaked from the finger of the beggar,
Time.[21]

The next few years proved difficult for MacLeish. Writing was still a passion, yet he hesitated to throw himself into it unconditionally. Letters from this period to family and friends, especially to his lifelong friend and Harvard law classmate Dean Acheson, show him struggling with indecision: "I took out my three pitiful shadows of careers—teaching, practice, journalism—and examined them individually and serially and in patterns till I was dizzy. . . . I discovered that my ambition to date has not been to do a certain work in the world but to be a certain person."[22] And: "No sooner than I determine upon one course, than the other beckons. . . . The result is that I have lost belief in myself and interest in my destiny. . . . A man's other career will live to haunt him."[23]

His single year of teaching coming to a close, MacLeish considered an offer from Roscoe Pound to teach at Harvard Law School, and declined. He appealed to Herbert Croley, editor of the *New Republic*, to take him on as a junior editor. But no offer was immediately forthcoming.[24] MacLeish then decided to accept a position with the Boston law firm of Choate, Hall & Stewart.[25] During the three years that followed, his life displayed many outward signs of success: a fine house in Cambridge,[26] a happy marriage,[27] children, an opportunity to teach law part time,[28] growing competence in trial practice,[29] and the prospect of a partnership.[30] Yet MacLeish was miserable; he found law grubby, most cases about whether $900,000 belonged this way or that, and not particularly socially useful.[31] To his parents he wrote: "The law is crowded—interesting—and full of despair. It offers its own rewards, but none other. Nothing that I would gladly be or have promises through its development. As a game there is nothing to match it. Even living is a poor second. But as a philosophy, as a training for such eternity as the next hour offers, it is nowhere—a mockery of human ambitions."[32] To his friend Dean Acheson: "My renewed interest in teaching results from no new enchantment with that profession, but from a profound suspicion of the practice of law. If I correctly analyze my emotions, I am attracted to the law by considerations the most superficial imaginable."[33] To his friend Bangs again: "I am now in the throes of deciding whether to stay on in the practice of law. . . . My ancient and misplaced ambition to write lies dreadfully at the bottom of it, for the whole purpose of the change would be more time for the concoction of words into verses. I wonder why I cling to that ambition so tenaciously."[34]

In an essay written years later, MacLeish recounts how he came to leave the practice of law.[35] After working late one cold night in February 1923, he walked, instead of taking his usual subway, from downtown Boston to his home in Cambridge. He was in crisis, his despair lit by the glare of the new moon. When he arrived home, he and his wife spent the entire night talking about their future. The next morning he went to the law firm to announce his resignation. The firm greeted him with the news that he had just been voted a partner.

The news did nothing to change his mind. He saw what was going on in America in the 1920s as "self indulgent . . . fat . . . rich . . . full of the most loathsome kinds of open and flagrant money-making. . . . To stay in America was . . . to practice art among hostiles and in the absence of mentors."[36] After selling their house and arranging their affairs, MacLeish, his wife Ada, and their two young children sailed for France on the S.S. *Lafayette* on 1 September 1923, bent on joining the same community of émigré writers that Pound had joined a few years earlier.[37] Like him, MacLeish had an indulgent father who supported his son's desire to write, but even more comfortably.[38] On the annual allowance of $3,000 that his father provided,[39] MacLeish's family was able to afford a governess,[40] a maid,[41] dinners out,[42] travel,[43] private schooling for their son,[44] and voice and music lessons with a famous teacher for Ada.[45] That teacher, Nadia Boulanger, and her sister Lily were none other than friends of Olga Rudge, Pound's mistress in Rapallo.[46]

Under his leaky skylight in Paris, at the age of thirty-one, MacLeish sat struggling with writer's block, realizing how much he had given up in the belief that he could become the poet he wished to be.[47] When the words would not come, he changed course and immersed himself in the study of English literature. He also taught himself enough French to read Rimbaud and the Symbolists, enough Italian to read Dante. He read Arthur Waley's translations of Li Po and other Chinese poets.[48] He read the literature of the past as he had read law at Harvard, seeking precedent and guidance for what he wanted to become. It took longer than either he or Ada had expected; neither of them spoke of it to the other.[49] Indeed, during this period MacLeish wrote to his former employer Charles Choate to inquire about resuming his career as a lawyer.[50] The inquiry went nowhere.

A sympathetic acquaintance, Amy Lowell, doyenne of American poetry, admonished him, "Do not simulate experience, plunge into it."[51] In time, he did. When the words started coming, he ventured out, eventually meeting most of the expatriate literary giants, including Hemingway, Fitzgerald, Joyce, and Dos Passos.[52] The MacLeishes were especially fond of Gerald and Sara Murphy, who were of the same social class and with whom they spent time together in the south of France.[53]

But much as Pound learned that one cannot come home again, MacLeish earned little more from his period in Paris than an enjoyable interlude. He began publishing in respectable presses and journals,[54] yet never gained full entrée into the inner circle of literary greats whose praise he sought. His ornate, rhetorical style put them off. They thought he was not a very good writer and had little original to say.[55] Moreover, MacLeish seemed too eager for acceptance. His letters to the other writers were "continuously laudatory."[56] He aped their manners, sprinkling expletives and tough talk in his letters to Hemingway while living comfortably in Paris sponsored by his wealthy father.[57] Privately, years later, he conceded that he and Ada turned out to be bad bohemians.[58] He also seemed too hungry for advice. For example, when John Peale Bishop suggested that he write about law, he produced a mundane poem, "Proprietor," about inheritance and the rule against perpetuities.[59]

But it was Pound who captivated MacLeish's attention and from whom he sought advice most anxiously.[60] He not only admired him for attacking the staid, over-ornate Victorian style of writing and opening the windows of stuffy Edwardian parlors,[61] even going so far as to write a maudlin poem in his honor.[62] He thought of Pound as an agent of change who was ushering in a new form of poetic organization. Before words can acquire fresh new meanings, he later wrote, "they must first be knocked free of the old mortar, pried loose from the old nails."[63] And Pound and a few other modernist poets were aiming to achieve just that.

Despite the praise that he showered on his would-be mentor, MacLeish received little in return. The more Pound criticized MacLeish, the more MacLeish sought his approval. Pound told him his work was derivative and that he would never amount to anything until he learned to write simply and without affectation.[64] He also told him: "The transparent devices to make a show of novelty are . . . not good enough. . . . If you have been [in Persia] GODDAMN it you ought precisely to make that felt."[65] In other letters, he called him "Artzimbaldo, the Vague."[66] MacLeish replied apologetically that he had come to writing late, weighed down "with a lot of accepted ideas," and "it's you I've got to get over."[67] Pound advised him to learn Arabic and Gaelic to give himself new perspective.[68]

MacLeish declined, but continued persevering at his poetry and seeking Pound's advice. After a while Pound relented and told him "one heave more, one crunch of the teeth and you ought to get through into your OWN."[69] But on other occasions, Pound spoke contemptuously about MacLeish to other poets.[70] MacLeish, however, did not hesitate to help Pound—perhaps because he hoped something would come of it. He sent Pound a check for $100 in 1927–28 to help keep afloat Pound's new periodical the *Exile*.[71] This was not the last time he would come to Pound's aid. In 1933 he made a financial contribution to help get Pound's *A Draft of Thirty Cantos* published in the United States.[72] And years later, after Pound's reversal of fortune, MacLeish sent money to Italy to help Pound with his fuel bills.[73] Little of this made an impression on Pound, who continued to treat MacLeish badly.[74]

Aware that his writing was producing diminishing returns, MacLeish returned to the United States with his family in 1928. After settling on a farm in Conway, Massachusetts, MacLeish wrote to friends and acquaintances about positions, finally accepting one at *Fortune* magazine which his friend Henry Luce had recently founded,[75] writing articles about finance and politics and composing poetry and essays in his free time.[76] The country was in hard times economically and jobs were scarce. MacLeish was fortunate that Luce, four years behind him at Yale and a fellow member of Skull and Bones, greatly admired him.[77] Indeed, when Luce started *Time* magazine in 1923, MacLeish had served as one of his many anonymous columnists, condensing news clippings from major newspapers.[78] In 1927, during a visit to Paris, Archie and Ada had hosted Luce and his wife.[79] When Luce, soon after, offered him the job at *Fortune*, MacLeish replied that he knew nothing about business. Luce responded, "That's why I want you," and offered him an arrangement allowing him to work as much as he needed and spend the rest of his time on his own writing.[80]

Under those favorable conditions, the grateful MacLeish was able to finish "Conquistador," his poem recounting the Spanish conquest of Mexico that eventually won a Pulitzer Prize.[81] The story differs from many accounts by highlighting the cruelty of the Spanish invaders who raped, murdered, and plundered the native people while pushing westward in search of more treasure. Pound weighed in again, accusing MacLeish of imitating his Cantos.[82] MacLeish's newfound sympathies with the underdog (new for his poetry, at any rate) undoubtedly built on some of the stories and articles he was writing for *Fortune* during this period, particularly about the nation's housing predicament.[83] MacLeish wrote dozens of articles and essays about financial hard times, the Depression, and the poverty that was haunting American workers.[84] Earlier he had flirted with communism, but he ultimately rejected it as rigid and anti-humanistic.[85] Now, he may have realized that a capitalist system needs more than impartial referees and a neutral system of laws, like a grand castle, to maintain itself.

One of MacLeish's articles during this period provided him the opportunity to explore both his newfound interest in Mexico and his concern for the hardships that runaway capitalism was imposing on workers and the poor. A blurb on Diego Rivera's *Frescoes of New York* in 1932, which appeared in *Fortune* magazine that year, quite possibly served as the starting point for *Frescoes for Mr. Rockefeller's City*, published in 1933, which sold as a chapbook published by the John Day Company for twenty-five cents apiece.[86] *Frescoes* is a curious hybrid: written in the florid, ornate, repetitive style for which Pound had criticized MacLeish earlier, it nevertheless goes on to show how capitalism has exploited American workers and artists. The poem drew sharp criticism from the New York literati for being patrician, condescending, and out of touch with the masses.[87] In an irony that would not come out until later, a columnist in the *New Republic* took MacLeish to task for being part of a group of "white-collar fascists out of Harvard and Wall Street."[88] Only a crystal ball would have caught the incongruity of the charge, for MacLeish's antithesis, Pound, was to be accused of pro-fascist broadcasts a few years later—charges against which MacLeish ultimately defended him.

Despite MacLeish's occasional displays of social sympathy and exposés of the evils of unvarnished laissez-faire capitalism, however, he, unlike some of his contemporaries in the literary movement, did not turn against the American class structure itself, much less against his own upper class. Instead, his writing during this period took the public turn that was to characterize much of his later work.[89] He became sermonic and hortatory, praising Felix Frankfurter, for example, for his commitment to republicanism and public service.[90] He wrote that despite its current troubles, American democracy was the hope of the world. His public turn, while helpful later to his government career, increasingly marginalized him from the literary establishment, some of whom had never forgiven him for "selling out" and taking the job with *Fortune* magazine.[91] Even though, during this period, MacLeish received critical acclaim and a Pulitzer Prize for "Conquistador," many of his old friends dismissed his recognition as undeserved.[92] What they perhaps failed to realize was that *Fortune* during the 1930s was a hotbed of leftists[93] and that many of MacLeish's writings during this period criticized laissez-faire capitalism and sided with the common man.[94]

MacLeish's estrangement from the old circle of leftist intellectuals and writers deepened with his publication a few years later of *The Irresponsibles*, a much-discussed monograph that seemed to accuse the writers of the 1920s of failing to see that the Second World War was not a replay of the first.[95] His friends saw the book as accusing them of moral apathy and of teaching the young that all convictions were fraudulent and that the United States was just one nation of many, with no special moral mission or destiny.[96] Earlier, MacLeish's friends had accused him of lacking a voice.

Now, some of them accused him of finding one—Americanism—which they decried. They also suspected him of opportunism and pointed out that his writing shifted with fads and changes in national consciousness.[97]

But MacLeish saw things a little differently. For him, the failure to see, speak out, and act against the threat of fascism to democracy was a product of a split in the creative community. By this he meant that the man of letters of the Jeffersonian eighteenth century was no more. Intellectual life had become specialized: A writer who takes the visual artist as his model creates and mirrors reality with little regard for moral truth. A scholar who studies the past takes for his model the research method of the scientists. Both writers and scientists shun value judgments about the worlds they create or describe.[98] The man of letters of the past, according to MacLeish, did not shun them but fearlessly engaged the issues of his day. For example, in "Public Speech and Private Speech in Poetry," he maintained that the greatest poets (for example, Milton and Dante) had been concerned with worldly issues. He also cited as examples of bad poetry the work of the Victorians ("teacup poets"), the Romantics, and the whisperers of the heart, ignoring that much of his earlier writing could be likened to theirs.[99] MacLeish might have approved of critics like Anthony Kronman, who urge that today's lawyers and legal educators seek solutions in the past to troubles gripping the professions today.[100] What we know is that he greatly approved of Felix Frankfurter's having brought legal realism to the Supreme Court,[101] and that he persevered in his position in the face of criticism, going so far as to "name names" in a second essay.[102]

Despite mixed reviews—even Yeats took issue with him in a poem titled "Politics"—MacLeish persevered with social commentary, oscillating between praising America and criticizing the excesses of its way of doing business.[103] By the end of the 1930s he had published three plays, *Panic*, *The Fall of the City*, and *Air Raid*.[104] The first, a Broadway play about an industrialist-banker who, on failing to save his bank, commits suicide, illustrates the conflict between capitalism and Marxism. The *New Republic* criticized it for being overly ideological and lacking any real characters.[105] *The Fall of the City* and *Air Raid* were radio plays predicting fascist victories and warning of the coming storm.

By the middle of the 1930s, MacLeish had turned away from his earlier preoccupation with self and the isolation of the individual[106] and joined the battle over fascism and communism. Indeed, he used that battle as a canvas on which to paint his vision of democracy for America. His growing love affair with democracy and abhorrence of fascism and collective movements in general eventually caused him to feel at odds with *Fortune* magazine, whose founder, Henry Luce, had taken a pro-Franco stance in the Spanish Civil War.[107] (He did not resign, however, until a broken romance and a new job offer spurred him to make a break.)[108] After eight years with the magazine and one as curator of the Nieman fellowship program for journalists at Harvard, he entered government service when Roosevelt appointed him Librarian of Congress, and a short time later director of the Office of War Information.[109] MacLeish interpreted his job as supplying news to the American people in a way that would inspire them to greater heights of war productivity.[110] Journalists distrusted him, demanding that he give them the news straight.[111] Perhaps one reason for their doubt was that he struck them as overly ideological and inclined to see the world in black and white terms. As his son put it, "In speeches and essays, Archie identified those he saw as enemies at home: 'The American defeatist who would rather lose the war . . . than make the terrible effort victory demands; the idle women whose dinner hours have been altered and who call their country's struggle for its life "this wretched war"; the sluggish men on the commuter trains who have never fought for anything but golf balls in their lives.'[112] He argued that defeatism could lead to a totalitarian takeover here, one that would have to be exceptionally brutal to control the people who had for so long been free."[113]

At this very period, Pound was making broadcasts in Italy attacking MacLeish and the American role in the war—actions that MacLeish found deeply troubling. He worshipped Pound the writer, but deplored his social views. In a letter in September 1943 to Harvey Bundy, assistant secretary of war and a former classmate, MacLeish conceded that Pound was a foolish man, but insisted that he was not a traitor. (MacLeish had, however, turned over to the FBI photographs of Pound taken in Paris in the early 1920s.)[114] He also suggested that if Pound were captured alive when the war ended, he could be returned to the United States for trial and then deported.[115] He also urged that Bundy issue an order that U.S. forces not summarily execute Pound when he was found, and instead return him to the United States for a civil trial.[116]

MacLeish's letters do not mention Pound again until May 1945. Having recently resigned as assistant secretary of state, MacLeish received an inquiry from T. S. Eliot asking what could be done for Pound. MacLeish briefed Eliot on Pound's situation and told him that if Pound were found to have accepted pay for his broadcasts, his only hope would be a defense based on "mitigating circumstances."[117]

In late 1945, MacLeish was appointed chair of the American delegation to the organizing conference of UNESCO, which took place in London from 1 to 16 November.[118] He was accordingly out of the country during the period immediately preceding Pound's return from Italy on 18 November. When MacLeish did return to the United States, Pound had been transferred from the District of Columbia jail to a local hospital for psychiatric evaluation.[119] In a letter to Pound's attorney, Julien Cornell, MacLeish said he would like to visit Pound, but hesitated to play any more active role in his defense: "As I told you when we first met, I find myself pulled in opposite directions by the whole Pound business. I have long admired him . . . as a poet. I have never thought his economics made any sense. . . . As for his broadcasts, if the excerpts I have seen published are typical, then I have only the most complete contempt."[120] On the same day, MacLeish wrote to Eliot: "I think I should say . . . that my feelings about this whole thing are increasingly mixed as I learn more about it. I shall be glad to do what I can . . . to see to it that Pound gets a fair trial . . . [and] to help as I can in getting him books and the things he needs. . . . [B]eyond that, I must reserve judgment."[121]

MacLeish did nothing to help Pound, nor did he visit him.[122] The insanity hearing had a foregone conclusion. Pound disappeared behind the asylum walls, just as MacLeish disappeared from public life. After the war, he returned to his home in Conway, where he fought depression and waited for the muse. As he put it later: "When I left Washington, I went to my farm . . . the weather was cold and wet and it sank into you, a damp wind streaming down from the golden Berkshires, and I tried to light a fire outside, but the wood was wet, the wood was green and would only smoke and sputter. It's just like me, I'm that way inside, I just won't burn inside."[123] MacLeish had not published a poem since he entered public service eight years earlier. His doubts about himself and the direction he should take heightened when he thought about the nation's obsession with international communism. The cold war had begun. The United States was caught up in xenophobia and nationalism. Although MacLeish loved his country—almost to a fault—he had little sympathy for the form that patriotism was taking during this period. He was particularly distressed by the House Un-American Activities Committee, which was holding hearings and examining the lives of citizens accused of harboring communist sympathies or associations.[124]

He emerged briefly from his self-imposed exile to chair the Lawrence Duggan fund, which had been set up to honor the work of a long-time State Department staffer and president of the Institute of International Education. Accused by the ex-communist Whitaker Chambers of providing information to America's enemies, Duggan fell to his death from the sixteenth-story window of his New York office. MacLeish was furious. Not only had Duggan suffered accusation by inference, but his work in furthering international understanding between cultures through student exchanges had come to an end. Though MacLeish had taken a passionate—even chauvinistic—stand for democracy and American values before and during the war, he could not go along with witch hunts, which he considered anathema to an open, democratic society.[125]

His convictions were to be tested again in 1949, when the Fellows of American Letters of the Library of Congress awarded Pound the first Bollingen Prize for poetry for *The Pisan Cantos*. Pound's friends, some of whom were on the committee, thought that the award would dramatize his situation and put pressure on the government to release him.[126] MacLeish, who had just been appointed Boylston Professor of Rhetoric and Oratory at Harvard,[127] defended the award by offering a spirited justification for Pound's place in American poetry, even though privately he believed that the *Cantos* were not among Pound's strongest works.[128]

His defense of Pound proved a turning point in MacLeish's life. In a short book entitled *Poetry and Opinion: The Pisan Cantos of Ezra Pound, A Dialog on the Role of Poetry*,[129] MacLeish rendered the issue into a debate between two characters representing Bollingen and the *Saturday Review of Literature*. The book features a lawyerly, formalist argument: "the question is not one of the childishness and perversity of Pound's political beliefs as they are expressed in this poem. The question is whether their expression here deprives the poems' insights of their meaning."[130]

At a period when his own poetry had fallen into eclipse, MacLeish harkened back to a rhetorical form learned in law school to defend the value of Pound's work, thus foreshadowing his role in bringing about the poet's release a few years later. Employing Aristotelian metaphors, he argued that Pound's poetry, by extolling fascism, served as a mirror of social currents—precisely the position against which MacLeish had railed only a short time earlier in *The Irresponsibles.*[131] Privately, MacLeish saw in Pound a brilliant man caught up in his time who made the wrong choices. MacLeish's concern in the Bollingen affair was to preserve the art of poetry in a free society, thinking that a democratic voice could be more easily silenced in a totalitarian state than the other way round.[132] He also believed that "nations are judged by the way they treat their artists" and that great artists deserve a measure of understanding and mercy.[133]

MacLeish's stand for artistic freedom later riled Joseph McCarthy, and he became one of the senator's most prominent targets[134] as well as one of his staunchest antagonists, joining with his colleagues at Harvard in defending the university against accusations that it was harboring communist sympathizers. For example, in explaining during his retirement speech years later what Harvard meant to him, MacLeish offered this:

> [It] was in Sanders Theatre late on a wet afternoon with a few professors on the wooden benches and a new President of the University on the stage with the Senior Fellows beside him and Dean of the Law School and a few more. There was no formality; no ceremony. Members of the Faculty had drawn up resolutions which they wished to present and did present—resolutions commending the courage of the University administration in standing wholly alone and without measurable public support against the most vicious menace to intellectual freedom in the history of Harvard—which means, in the history of the country. The resolutions had no authority but the authority of the names signed to them—professors' names. The event had no public recognition: No reporter was there or would have found anything to report if he had been. But in that almost empty room and in that failing light there was the presence of the thing we mean.[135]

The Bollingen controversy soon faded from national consciousness. The Truman Doctrine—aid to Greece and Turkey to fight indigenous communism—led to the cold war and then the undeclared war in Korea, which was supported by both conservatives and liberals.[136] McCarthyism swept the land. Although MacLeish had left government service for Harvard, he feared, realistically, that he might become an even greater target and so was probably reluctant to give McCarthy any additional ammunition. At any rate, he took measures to distance himself from any taint.[137]

After McCarthy was censured, MacLeish resumed writing to Pound.[138] In three letters written in the fall of 1955, MacLeish referred to his earlier promise of a visit, offered to see Pound when he was next in Washington, queried him about an acceptable solution to his situation, and reminded him that he had little influence with the Republicans but would do what he could.[139] In one of his letters, MacLeish wrote, "I will do what I can and try to instigate others who can do more. I don't mean by this, organization or, least of all, publicity. I mean the only kind of action that really counts—individual action in individual terms."[140] (MacLeish, of course, ended up doing much more than that.)

In December 1955, ten years after Pound entered St. Elizabeths, MacLeish visited him there. Afterward, he wrote: "Not everyone has seen Pound in the long, dim corridor inhabited by the ghosts of men who cannot be still, or who can be still too long. . . . When a conscious mind capable of the most complete human awareness is incarcerated among minds which are not conscious and cannot be aware, the enforced association produces a horror which is not relieved either by the intelligence of doctors of by the tact of administrators or even by the patience and kindliness of the man who suffers it. You carry the horror away and whenever afterward you think of Pound or read his lines a stale sorrow afflicts you."[141]

After the visit, MacLeish worked tirelessly over a two-year period to mobilize support for Pound.[142] He wrote to his longtime friend Hemingway[143] and spoke with T. S. Eliot in London.[144] He wrote repeatedly to Robert Frost, then eighty-three, cajoling him into making the long train trip from Vermont to meet with him and Attorney General William P. Rogers.[145] He wrote to Dag Hammarskjöld (secretary general of the United Nations),[146] William J. Fulbright,[147] Christian Herter (undersecretary of state),[148] Milton Eisenhower,[149] and many others. MacLeish even used reverse psychology, planting the thought in Frost's mind that Pound was getting too much publicity, and that if they got him out he would receive less.[150] (Frost considered himself a rival of Pound for public attention.) MacLeish's assessment of Frost's egotism proved true when later, after Pound's release, Frost declared with some satisfaction that Pound would now receive less attention. How ironic, then, that Frost received much of the credit for MacLeish's behind-the-scenes efforts.

Those efforts finally bore fruit. Pound received a new hearing on 18 April 1958 and was ordered released.[151] Within two months, Pound and his wife Dorothy set sail for Italy, where he remained until his death in 1972, silent,[152] increasingly lonely, and finally repentant.[153]

MacLeish's Role in the Pound Affair

Conventional explanations of MacLeish's role in the Pound affair rest either on sympathy or public calling: MacLeish rescued Pound because he empathized with the embattled poet, or because he wanted to spare his country the embarrassment of Pound's continued incarceration.[154] Although both explanations contain an element of truth, they are insufficient. In particular, neither can easily account for the changes in Mac-Leish's position—responding at first coolly to Pound and even urging that he be deported, then riding to his rescue ten years later. A more complete account requires a closer look into MacLeish's divided character, his relationship to political power in the United States during the Second World War and the postwar period—and, more basically, the shifting concepts of law and legal education.

Sympathy and Partisan Politics   Sympathy alone, while it certainly played a part, cannot explain MacLeish's actions. Sympathy presumably would have been most acute in 1945 and 1946, when Pound first faced treason charges, and then an uncertain future in an insane asylum, not ten years later when Pound had seemingly adjusted to his situation. By the same token, partisan politics offers no better explanation. In 1945 MacLeish was a highly placed figure in a Democratic administration. By 1955, however, the country was in the hands of the Republicans. Sympathy and politics do come into play in explaining MacLeish's behavior toward Pound, but they interact in complex ways and are mediated, as we shall see, by MacLeish's character and class loyalties.

Vicarious Satisfaction MacLeish was a fine lawyer, technically skilled and blessed with a powerful persona, yet he always hungered for literature. Trained in English and the humanities, he found the practice of law narrow, technical, dull—and a little grubby. Life in the firm was strenuous, consuming most of his energy and time. He wrote little and his letters express his longing for poetry and art. Yet when he mustered his courage to move to Paris, life there failed to satisfy his expectations as well. Rather than continue his relatively spartan existence, he returned to the United States, upper-class life, and a succession of safe jobs, writing creatively on the side.

Aided by personal connections and his own considerable talents, MacLeish moved up in the world, ultimately winning appointment as assistant secretary of state under Roosevelt.[155] Yet his public turn took him even further from the world of poetry and must have deepened his estrangement from his literary self. Later in life, with his public career at its zenith and his writing career stalled, the specter of Pound, aging and still imprisoned, reentered MacLeish's life. The politics of the time had changed, and a group of Pound's friends and supporters were beginning to talk about his release.

Why did MacLeish, public servant, reach back for his rusty legal talents and put them to effective use to free Pound?[156] Perhaps he was in part seeking personal fulfillment—satisfaction of his own yearning for the life of a writer, the life Pound had had. By saving Pound, MacLeish could achieve vicariously that which he himself had allowed to drift away. In rescuing Pound, MacLeish rescued himself, attaining psychological and personal integration and a sense of closure. Even his long-abandoned legal career took on new meaning; his skills as lawyer and advocate brought about Pound's release. Through Pound's rescue, MacLeish vindicated a life of virtuous compromise—the half-lawyer, half-poet was able to achieve something unique. If he could not be a man of genius, at least he could rescue someone who was.[157]

The Role of Class Interest Freeing Pound therefore must have attracted MacLeish for personal reasons. But MacLeish was also a public man, who had advanced steadily to become a high-ranking member of the eastern liberal political establishment.[158] At the time of Pound's commitment, the interests of that establishment required his confinement. Pound was a national embarrassment, his racist, anti-Semitic, and pro-fascist statements antithetical to the official attitudes underlying our war effort and early cold war positions.

By 1955, however, Pound had been committed for nearly ten years and was nearing the end of his life. Death in an asylum would have reflected poorly on the United States—her greatest living poet spending his last years behind bars.[159] Moreover, Pound's literary reputation had unexpectedly risen while he was in St. Elizabeths. The chief psychiatrist had taken a liking to him, basking in the attention received indirectly from his famous patient. He provided a supportive atmosphere, juggling reports and statements to maintain the fiction that his inmate was slightly too crazy to stand trial again.[160] All of Pound's creature comforts received attention, including a succession of young women who visited him alone in his quarters.[161]

At the same time, the danger represented by Pound's extremist views had abated. The wartime horror of fascism had receded; McCarthy had been censured.[162] Hemingway and other literary figures were beginning to speak out on Pound's behalf.[163] *Brown v. Board of Education*[164] and other symbolic victories had reassured many blacks that the country had their interests at heart. The balance of interests had shifted—MacLeish and his class could safely release Pound.[165] Ironically, when Thurgood Marshall, representing the NAACP, persuaded the Supreme Court to declare a ringing victory for racial justice in *Brown*, the resulting softening of social attitudes allowed the United States to release her most famous Aryan supremacist without forfeiting cold war leadership.[166] The most impressive black lawyer of his time may have set the stage for the release of one of America's most talented racist anti-Semites.

MacLeish, then, served as the instrument of social forces that he might not at the time have perceived. Yet by a kind of sure instinct bred at Hotchkiss, Yale, and Harvard, MacLeish knew what America's interests dictated and acted accordingly.

The Role of Legal Formalism   MacLeish received a legal education steeped in legal formalism, which tries to make law a science, reducing human factors and fact patterns to fit precedent, minimizing the role of judgment, politics, compassion, and discretion.[167] Later sections of this book trace the story of what this conception of law can do to a lawyer. We show how dissatisfaction begins for many with law school, and how the demands of legal practice—billable hours, narrow specialization, and the pressures of partnership—merely amplify that dissatisfaction. The reader will see how lawyers' discontent with their own work finds a counterpart in the public's disenchantment with driven, self-absorbed professionals who do not communicate and like nothing better than to fight.

MacLeish could even be seen as foreshadowing the current narrative school of antiformalist legal scholarship, whose adherents include such descendents of legal realism and critical legal studies as Patricia Williams and Derrick Bell, who like him have tried to break free from the constraints of doctrine and law as science. Unlike them MacLeish had no particular political agenda—at least in his early years. He merely wanted law to be something more than cases and precedent. His legal education did not satisfy his soul, his longings for richness and texture. A little like certain contemporary critics, his teachers at Harvard taught him to put aside youthful ways. Born a little too soon, he missed, by just a few years, the flowering of legal realism and interdisciplinary law at Harvard and elsewhere.[168]

Drawing on the story of Archibald MacLeish and Ezra Pound, we show that lawyers' unhappiness contains both a conceptual dimension, concerned with how they understand what they do, and a phenomenological one that embraces the felt experiences of law and lawyering. MacLeish's predicament, it turns out, has roots in an approach to law and legal practice known as formalism. We make the case, on both theoretical and psychological grounds, for critical theory as a countermeasure to the professional dissatisfaction gripping the legal profession today.

This is not to say that professional life should be free flowing and lacking in discipline. All thought requires order and a degree of rigor. Pound, one of life's great anarchists, needed someone like MacLeish to bring to his life a semblance of order. But society today must learn to appreciate narrative, richness, even disorder, just as we welcome formalism, predictability, and mechanical jurisprudence. Particularly during times of social change, rules laid down during an earlier period, when women, blacks, and workers, for example, knew their place, may disserve society just as law school and practice failed to satisfy MacLeish. Formalism and repetition cause one to examine the case at hand only for those features that render it similar to some prior one. New stories, new aspects of justice, are marginalized, sometimes to our detriment. Formalism also imposes unbearable pressures on creative, high-spirited human beings. MacLeish, an uncommonly brilliant and good man raised on legal and literary formalism, could not resolve those pressures. Here we are half a century later. Are we doing much better?

11 Discontents

The law has one way of seeing. . . .

Poetry has another. But the journey is the same.

—Archibald MacLeish,

Apologia (1972)

3 Formalism

Earlier we posited that the unhappy MacLeish came to law too soon for someone of his broad range of interests. Entering law school just before the revolution of the 1920s swept aside the reigning mechanical jurisprudence, MacLeish missed out on the broader vision of law and legal practice that the legal realists introduced. Instead, he received an education steeped in legal formalism, which emphasizes rules, principles, and cases laid out in abstract, orderly systems.[1]

Before examining the discontents of today's lawyers, it is instructive to take a look at MacLeish's legal world as he first encountered it at Harvard. What is legal formalism, the approach that dominated law then and is resurgent today? What about legal realism and its contemporary incarnations, critical legal studies, feminist legal theory, and critical race theory? And finally, what do these approaches, seemingly operating at a level of high theory, have to do with unhappy lawyers and angry clients? Do they find counterparts in the world of work, so that the way a profession conceives of itself, intellectually, is apt to go along with a particular set of disciplinary rules, expectations, and office practices?

This part of the book briefly defines terms such as formalism and its many opposites, including legal realism, and sets out our thesis in somewhat greater detail. We paint here with a broad brush, seeking not perfect proof but rather a story or narrative that will resonate with the reader, who may have encountered something similar in his or her life. The following sections of the book examine the discontents of two professions in greater detail. The reader looking for something akin to proof—or, at least, persuasion—may perhaps find it there.

Legal Formalism

Our examination of MacLeish's life revealed an intelligent man with liberal social instincts who found his profession confining and stifling. His personal correspondence and occasional formal writing exhibited growing dissatisfaction with law's aridity, lack of intellectual content, and inability to serve the common good. MacLeish lacked the conceptual tools to name the source of his discontent. But he knew something was wrong. Was it law's incessant demands? The way it seemed to exclude intuition, imagination, and human values? The way practice was structured? Or was it simply that he loved something else—literature—more, so that law, like any other calling, consumed the time and energy he would have liked to devote to writing? That he might have found most of what he was looking for in one career seemed never to have occurred to the young lawyer, any more than it did to most of his contemporaries or does to many current law students who study under narrow curricula, graduate, and go on to careers that leave them wondering whether they could have done better.

If, as we contend, the worm at the heart of MacLeish's discontent was legal formalism, what do we mean by the term? Formalism is used in many different senses and can assume diverse meanings in different disciplines and settings. Even in law it carries a variety of meanings.[2] But what we mean by the term is a conception of legal reasoning that emphasizes internal rather than external factors in generating legal decisions.[3] Legal formalism emphasizes precedent—what a court decided yesterday—rather than social policy and the search for an answer that would be right for today.[4] In formalism, a legal decision is apt to turn on categorical questions—what kind of case is this? Does it concern a particular power, such as Congress's ability to enact laws regulating interstate commerce? Does it present an issue of equal protection, in which case a court must afford it either strict or lax scrutiny, depending on the type of discrimination that has taken place? Is a fundamental interest such as privacy or the right to interstate travel present, and if so has the state invaded that right only upon adequate justification and in a way calculated to infringe it as little as possible?[5]

For formalism, justice is a matter of regularity and predictability. And these virtues are best assured by confining the decision maker to a relatively small number of matters or "elements," ideally of an easily ascertained sort. "It's this kind of case. So, I must apply this rule, and only material elements A, B, and C (duty, breach, and causation) are relevant, and not D, E, F, and G."[6] Formalism is a rule of exclusion. Life, however, is diverse and unruly. New cases arise all the time. A familiar-looking case may present elements A, B, and C, yet something about this defendant or setting may argue for a different result. Our sense of justice may rankle—the result, while right in the "landmark" legal case that handed down the rule, may seem wrong now. Legal formalism says that does not matter.[7]

Legal Formalism and the Law Schools:
How Lawyers Are Trained

Legal formalism is associated with a form of education that emphasizes doctrines and cases and minimizes external factors, such as justice, social policy, and politics. It imagines law as an autonomous discipline existing apart from others; it is not at all interdisciplinary.[8] The classroom is Socratic and doctrinal. The professor asks what the rule of the case is and how it squares with that of a previous one. He or she asks how the case would come out if one of the facts were different, say, if the defendant were a child. (The student is supposed to remember that a different rule comes in.) The beginner may attempt to answer by resort to morality or justice: "The plaintiff should win because the defendant was a bad person and it would be wrong for the plaintiff, who will go through life as a cripple, to walk away with nothing." The professor will dismiss such answers as dangerously naïve. The student soon learns to give the right—legalistic—response: "According to such and such a case, the plaintiff will lose, because. . . ." (although a bright student might argue that a different rule might apply or that the addition of one single new fact might change the seemingly harsh result).

History of Formalism:
How a Peculiar Approach Got Started

To the average reader, it might appear strange that legal education is so narrow and confined. Law, after all, is a broad discipline touching on an extremely wide range of human activity. Formalist pedagogy and theory, however, seek to impose a simplified grid on a chaotic, diverse reality, akin to trying to explain all of physics by one or two simple rules, such as those of classical kinetics.[9] How did this approach come to dominate American law schools, and why does it exert such a strong hold even today?

During most of the first century of this country's history, there were no law schools as such. Lawyers learned their craft by the apprenticeship method. They "read the law," receiving instruction and tutelage in the office of a local practitioner who trained and taught them until they were deemed ready to enter practice.[10] Abraham Lincoln, for example, learned law this way. Then, near the end of the nineteenth century, American universities began opening "departments" of law. These new additions at first lacked legitimacy. Professors in other departments, such as history, sociology, and political science, looked down on their new colleagues, considering them no more than slightly elevated practitioners who drilled students by rote (which they did) and lacked any interesting theoretical or intellectual understanding of their discipline or of anything else.[11]

Just at that moment, as though by magic, appeared a reformer. Christopher Columbus Langdell, professor of law at Harvard Law School, preached a new method and theory of legal education. His students pored over masses of cases—appellate decisions in which judges set out the reasoning by which they arrived at certain results—in search of principles of law that the students were expected to organize into a coherent, hierarchical system.[12] The hundreds of cases studied in a particular class, such as torts, were like materials in a laboratory, which the students examined and out of which they distilled principles of law. Now a branch of inductive science, like physics or chemistry, law became respectable and the new departments discovered their reason for being. Endowed with fresh credibility and an unimpeachable mission, law professors could now hold their own at the faculty club.[13]

The Legal Realist Revolution

Mechanical jurisprudence and doctrinalism reigned for a few decades, just long enough for the fledging law schools to establish themselves within the university. Then, a group of radical reformers including Oliver Wendell Holmes and Roscoe Pound, and later Morris Cohen, Jerome Frank, and

Karl Llewellyn, became dissatisfied with this approach to law. Not only was formalism desiccated, they pointed out, but it was impossible to actually decide cases that way. Every legal rule was susceptible to a multitude of interpretations. It meant nothing until actually interpreted by a judge or other empowered actor in response to a particular situation. And when a judge did approach a specific set of facts, he always brought into the evaluation a host of factors, most unstated, in addition to the various competing principles or rules that could just as easily bear upon them. These other factors included the judge's political or social loyalties or commitments, his sense of what the broader society—or the business community, or the ruling élite—needed. They included the judge's preferences for this or that form of social ordering—even his mood on that occasion and reaction, visceral or not, to the litigants.[14]

Realism Spreads and Sparks Successor Movements

Widely recognized as a movement whose time had come, legal realism took the law schools by storm. Mechanical jurisprudence fell into disuse—except in a few redoubts such as the Supreme Court, which continued to ignore realism's teachings for a critical decade or two—replaced by a host of modern movements, including the law and society movement. That collection of scholars, centered at the University of Wisconsin law school, emphasized law in action as opposed to law on the books. They studied jury behavior, judicial discretion, and why the haves always seem to come out ahead. Liberal in its orientation, the law and society movement supplied the breeding ground for critical legal studies ("crit" theory), an even more radical departure from orthodoxy that took hold in the late 1960s and early 1970s. Figures such as Duncan Kennedy, Richard Abel, Peter Gabel, Morton Horowitz, and Roberto Unger taught that law was indeterminate and that every legal problem had more than one right answer. They wrote about the role of hierarchy in the law and the way in which capitalist institutions subtly bend law to their bidding. They wrote about how many law students begin with progressive aspirations but change into hired guns capable, emotionally, of arguing either side of a case, and how American substantive law reflects the values of early English mercantilism.[15]

Critical legal studies, in turn, spurred the development of radical feminist approaches to law, which applied power and hegemony analysis to patriarchy and gender relations, and critical race theory, which sought to understand how a formally race-neutral system of laws methodically subordinated minorities.[16]

Formalism Endures

Although each of these progressive movements counts adherents across the country, and although virtually every legal academic has adopted some tenets and vocabulary from at least one of the movements, formalism retains a strong hold on legal education. Still considered the paradigm, Socratic teaching enables a single professor to wield control over a large classroom of one hundred or more students.[17] It is not only cost-effective: professors with the verve and stage presence to deploy the Socratic method effectively command the students' respect—students consider them a dying breed. Such professors really do teach you something. They demand performance—you had better be on your toes. They teach "real law," as opposed to the amorphous collection of maxims known as social policy or the politically tinged admonitions of the crits and critical race theorists. For a short time in the middle of the twentieth century, the Warren Court was reformist and willing to consider a host of factors—equity, evolving standards of conscience, the historical background of a case—on the way to a decision.[18] The opinions of more recent courts display the formalism of a hornbook—those collections of black-letter laws and rules that students use to bone up for an examination—even when deciding cases of great social importance.[19] Society as a whole became more conservative; courts found it easy, under the banner of legalism, to follow suit. While many in the legal academy pay lip service to notions such as indeterminacy, formalism is as entrenched as it has been at any time since Christopher Columbus Langdell.

This latter-day formalism has attracted a school of academic defenders and apologists who urge, for example, that law can only be understood from a vantage point within it—only there does its inner intelligibility come into view.[20] Others reason that formalism is concerned with the idea of restraint and the notion that judges are forbidden to substitute their own values for settled law,[21] or that rationality and precedent are what we mean by the rule of law—a system of rules that we agree to observe in the expectation that others will do likewise.[22] That system gives law its legitimacy while guarding against the anarchy that might reign without it.[23]

Legal Practice and Education Follow Suit

Just as legal formalism began its comeback, the structure of legal practice changed, as well.[24] Formalism turned out to offer much the same cost-effectiveness in legal practice as it did in teaching. Beginning around 1960, practice became disciplined, routinized, compartmentalized, and result-driven; lawyers, highly accountable for their time. Legal specialization and hierarchy increased, and a well-defined law firm structure developed with the partners at the top and a host of anxious associates at the bottom, toiling long hours in the hopes of attracting the attention of the partners and securing a partnership of their own. Legal education became more competitive as the pool of highly qualified applicants grew with the Watergate scandal, the popularity of TV programs starring lawyers, the dearth of jobs for graduates of humanities programs, and the downturn in certain sectors of the U.S. economy. Making law review and getting the right judicial clerkship came to be seen as the route to a good job, high salary, and prestigious career. Law classes, which were huge, were graded based on a single, three-hour essay examination at the end of the term. A facility in manipulating cases and doctrines came to be seen as virtuosity par excellence and a security blanket for the time-stressed law student.

The Politics of Formalism

Formalism could theoretically be of the political left or right variety.[25] But in practice it came to be aligned with a soft form of conservatism, which at times developed a sharp edge. As was noted earlier, formalism emphasizes the rule of precedent, which is bound up with the past. It slows the pace of change, assuring that things remain the way they were longer than they might if we were free to make departures when conditions changed. Formalism simply assumes that the existing set of rules is necessary and right, ignoring that they were probably enacted to serve the interests of the ruling class. Moreover, in denying the relevance of power, formalism camouflages the way power actually works, so that it can get its way with even less dissent than usual.

Formalism also reduces the number of considerations a court may take into account—equity, mercy, economics, and class relations, just to name a few. Formalistic legal decisions tend to have an abstract, bloodless quality, devoid of the gritty details of defendants who killed their mothers or white supremacists who burned crosses in the yards of black families. (The case turns instead on First Amendment theory and the nature of the municipal ordinance forbidding racial harassment.)[26] Yet it is concrete detail that tends to kindle conscience and call on us to say, "That result is unjust"—to remind us, as one legal scholar put it, that courts write in a field of pain and death.[27] In fact, a competing system—equity—developed because of the very limitations of early Anglo-American law. A court of equity could step in and "do equity" when legal remedies, such as damages, were inadequate. The court could craft innovative approaches, such as an accounting or an injunction, to avoid the wooden, formulaic quality of age-old categories such as trespass and assumpsit.

Before the legal realist revolution, judges professed to be applying law in a neutral, value-free manner. A prince and a pauper, the state and the dissenter, would receive the same treatment. The approach was mechanical, logical, and deductive. Opinions were thought to take the form of a grand syllogism: here is the law, here the facts; applying the law to these facts, we reach this result. Indeed this approach was equated with legal virtue: justice was blind. The realists introduced skepticism into that neat picture, arguing that judges do not—perhaps cannot—proceed in such a fashion. Many different rules may apply to a given case, each pointing in a different direction. No meta-rule tells a judge which one to select. In the absence of formal determinacy, judges bring to bear a host of background considerations—class preferences, personal predilections, and ingrained habits—in reaching a result. Judges ought to reject the pretense of neutrality and straightforwardly render decisions aimed at making the world a better place.

Plessy v. Ferguson

Before this realist view gained currency, the legal system rendered a number of decisions that can only be described as perverse. In 1896 the Supreme Court considered one of many Jim Crow laws by which southern states sought to roll back black gains achieved during the short-lived period known as Reconstruction. When a light-skinned African American challenged such a measure—a law requiring separate railroad cars for blacks and whites—the Supreme Court upheld it against a challenge that it violated equal protection.[28] The cars were formally equal, the Court wrote, and the law requires nothing more. To the idea that separate seating areas were an insult to one race—the black—but not the other, the Court turned a deaf ear; that complaint had to do with social practices, not law. Separate facilities were an insult only if blacks chose to place that interpretation on them. For the Court, only one fact mattered—that the two cars were functionally equal. The decision initiated an era, lasting nearly sixty years, of separate schooling, public swimming pools, and many other facilities for African Americans—facilities that often were equal in name only to those provided to whites.

Lochner v. New York

A few years later, the U.S. Supreme Court considered a challenge to a New York law limiting the number of hours that bakery employees could work to ten per day, or sixty a week. The legislature had enacted the law after listening to evidence of widespread abuses in the industry, including dangerous workplace conditions and forced labor. After hearing argument from both sides, the Court invalidated the law as impairing freedom of contract.[29] Workers were free to accept or reject onerous conditions of work, just as employers were free to find workers who would tolerate them. Each side was free to contract—the worker, to sell his or her labor on whatever terms he or she could command; the employer, to offer jobs to those who suited him. Perfect symmetry. The problem, of course, which the New York legislature recognized, is that the positions of worker and employer are not symmetrical. The worker needs a job to earn the necessities of life. The employer needs the job filled, but if it is not filled by one worker, another will come along. The business will go on.

Lochner struck down New York's regulatory scheme by seeing the case in starkly narrow terms—liberty of contract. Considerations such as social welfare, the health of the labor market, protection of children and families, and the right to a decent livelihood did not enter the picture. The decision solidified corporate power at the expense of the working poor. At the time the Supreme Court decided *Lochner*, workplace safety was so abysmal, and corporate profits so great, that the period has come to be known, ironically, as the Gilded Age. Fatalities in industries such as textiles ran high; one-third of workers did not live to see their twenty-fifth birthday.[30] The courts employed abstract doctrines such as freedom of contract to strike down one worker protection law after another, ignoring that freedom meant one thing to an impoverished worker and another to a capitalist. But the values that produced cases like *Lochner* protected industrialists for only a short period. Eventually they plunged the country into a devastating depression. They even prevented Franklin Roosevelt's administration from enacting measures to combat the downturn, until the president threatened to pack the Court by appointing additional, more sympathetic Justices to it. The Court then began upholding social legislation in cases like *West Coast Hotel v. Parrish*[31] (which upheld a law setting minimum wages for women and children in the state of Washington). The victory over Lochnerism was to prove short-lived, however.

Brown v. Board of Education and
Neutral Principles of Constitutional Law

In 1954 the Supreme Court decided a group of cases challenging the separate-but-equal doctrine of *Plessy v. Ferguson* in a new setting: segregated schools. Southern school districts had been routinely assigning black schoolchildren to one, usually run-down, school, and whites to another, better funded and equipped, under the guise of operating "separate but equal" schools.[32] Some administrators justified this approach paternalistically: the black schoolchildren were said to lack the intellectual capacity or background to compete with their better prepared white counterparts. Separate schools were allegedly in the best interest of the black children, who would learn under conditions more suited to their abilities. Some school districts in the North and the Midwest adopted the same rationalization.

In *Brown*, the Supreme Court held that racially segregated pupil assignment schemes violated the guarantee of equal protection inherent in the Fourteenth Amendment.[33] Separate schools for black and white children can never be equal, the Supreme Court said, because society will ascribe one meaning to the white schools and another to the black. The black schoolchildren will internalize that meaning, realize that society deems them unfit to learn with the white children, and suffer permanent psychological harm as a result. *Brown* thereby assigned *Plessy v. Ferguson* and its formalistic rule to the scrap heap of history.

But the decision did little, by itself, to change the social attitudes that had supported separate-but-equal schooling all along. School administrators in much of the South went on acting as they had before, devising ways to frustrate the mandate of *Brown*.[34] Even in the North, the racial makeup of most schools remained the same, as white parents withdrew their children from schools under desegregation orders, or moved to the suburbs.[35] If the blacks are free to send their children to the school they choose, these parents seemed to reason, so are we: Legal Formalism 101. Those few who read the law reviews soon received support in the form of a famous essay in the *Harvard Law Review*. Written by the liberal scholar Herbert Wechsler, the essay lamented how the Supreme Court had casually sacrificed the associational rights of whites in favor of those of blacks. Why were blacks free to associate with whites when whites were not similarly free *not* to associate with blacks?

The Justices of the Supreme Court (on whose minds associational rights were the last thing) provided no answer to this question. Wechsler's article, entitled "Toward Neutral Principles of Constitutional Law,"[36] pronounced the *Brown* decision unprincipled. Of course, no legal principle compelled school desegregation. One could examine cases and doctrines forever and not find one disclosing that sending all the black children to school in a closet would be socially damaging. It is social knowledge that tells us this; everyone who lives in our world knows it. "The life of the law is not logic, but experience," Oliver Wendell Holmes, an early realist, once wrote.[37] Wechsler's error demonstrates how little one can achieve by logic and syllogistic reasoning alone. Sometimes law must look to other sources of information, intuition, common sense, and prudential knowledge. Sometimes one must even look to great literature, which has always struggled with fundamental questions.[38] This is why we say MacLeish was born a little too soon. Think what his life might have been like had his prodigious intellect received its early schooling from Karl Llewellyn, William

Hastie (architect of *Brown v. Board of Education*), or the later generation of realists, critical scholars, and interdisciplinary thinkers. What a formidable—not to mention happier—lawyer he might have been!

Lochnerism Today: Legal Formalism Resurges

It would be easy to conclude that legal realism and critical thought changed legal education and the practice of law for all time. But they did not. They do embolden those lawyers and scholars who prefer to address the broad social or humanistic dimensions of their discipline. But formalism remains the dominant self-understanding of law schools and the practicing bar. And as we shall see, its emphasis on text and precedent greatly appeals to the world of corporate clients as well.

Legal Education Legal education today features two powerful currents, both with strong formalist overtones. One is the critique emanating from the MacCrate Report and Judge Harry Edwards that legal education and scholarship are not practical enough. Commissioned by the American Bar Association to examine the contents of legal education, a committee headed by the prominent lawyer Robert MacCrate recommended a return to practical, skills-based training with an emphasis on legal writing, interviewing, the form of legal citation, and skills such as filing briefs and keeping good records.[39] Greeted with praise by traditionalists and teachers of doctrine, the report proved highly influential. Most law schools changed their course offerings in the direction it suggested.

Shortly after the report appeared, a second bombshell went off when Edwards, a federal appellate judge and former member of the University of Michigan law faculty, published a sharp critique of modern legal scholarship. Entitled "The Growing Disjunction between Legal Education and the Legal Profession,"[40] his article took legal scholarship to task as overly theoretical and of little use to judges and the practicing bar.[41] Like the MacCrate Report, his article found little to praise in theory, criticism, the law and literature movement, or writing aimed at understanding the broad social dimensions of law. "Pay attention to us and our needs," the report and article seemed to say. "Never mind that new theory. Give me the citation and the line of cases I need right now." Of course, many (perhaps most) legal scholars had been doing this all along, writing ponderous, 120-page law review articles with hundreds of footnotes analyzing judicial trends. The two reports reinforced what they were doing and discouraged critical scholars, postmodernists, and promulgators of theory.

The Supreme Court   Except for a brief period in the 1960s and 1970s, the Supreme Court has not been particularly receptive to progressive social thought or even interdisciplinary analysis of, for example, the racial impact of the death penalty.[42] Today, it is even more formalistic, technical, and otherworldly than usual. Republican presidents have loaded the Court with technocrats, to the point where many writers have concluded that Lochnerian reasoning has returned.[43] Certainly, the broad vistas and social engagement of the New Deal era and the Warren Court are no longer in evidence. Under the banners of federalism, original intent, and extreme textualism, the Court has been issuing a series of opinions narrowing the scope of state and federal authority to act for the common good and reversing lower court opinions that deviated from the most crabbed interpretation of precedent and legislative text.[44] A good illustration is a string of cases, reminiscent of *Plessy v. Ferguson*, in which the Supreme Court under the banner of constitutional color blindness invalidated affirmative action rules giving African Americans and other minorities access to job markets from which they had been explicitly excluded. Reinterpreting the mandate against racial discrimination to include measures that disadvantage historically advantaged groups such as white males, the Court in *Wards Cove Packing Co. v. Antonio*[45] and *City of Richmond v. J. A. Croson Co.*[46] struck down workplace rules designed to afford entry to minorities.

In a major challenge to discriminatory administration of the death penalty, the Court rejected statistical proof that blacks who kill whites are executed at many times the rate of whites who kill blacks. Those statistics are irrelevant, the Court held, because they do not show that the disparity was produced by a conscious intent. And in the absence of proof that particular jurors or prosecutors harbored racist designs, the disproportion could have come about in many ways, including chance.[47]

Legal Practice   Just as legal education and the judiciary have rigidified, the structure of legal practice has followed suit. The routinization that put off the intellectually adventurous MacLeish has increased manyfold. Lawyers specialize, and even within specialties (such as securities, real estate, or corporate law), big-firm lawyers carve cases up into small parts, so that few attorneys have much client contact or get a chance to see the big picture. A young associate fresh out of law school can spend months, even years, in the back corner of the library researching damages in a single big case, or going through thousands of pages of documents obtained in the course of discovery, organizing the material and looking for patterns. Pressure to generate billable hours has increased, while competition for partnership has become even keener than before. Lawyers have little leisure time to think about their cases, much less for family or recreational pursuits. The days of the attorney as a wise counselor have largely passed. Law is a business. And that business is to sell technical advice at the highest price possible.

Let us now look into the world of the lawyer a little more closely.

4 Lawyers and Their Discontents

It was early in her second month as a new associate at Plimpton, Day, Regan, and Berringer, and Georgina Barras was already wondering whether she had not made a serious mistake. It was not just the long subway ride from her nicely appointed apartment on the other side of town, nor even the ten-hour days she found it necessary to put in to keep abreast of the work. It was more than that. She made a note to make a list sometime of all the things that were bothering her and think about it. But there was so little time, even for taking stock. Maybe she should have taken that job in the small firm, or the other one that they had offered her, as a top graduate of one of the nation's leading schools, doing public-interest work. But her student loans were so large—and her salary at the firm so high. She'd be able to pay off her obligations in just a few years, and maybe afford a down payment on that condo that she and her fiancé, Dan, had had their eyes on. Setting her face and turning on her computer, she sighed and started the new day.

Why are lawyers so discontented? How deep does that discontent run, and how much of it is attributable to formalism? If, as we suspect, a great deal is, then what is the solution? More training in legal ethics, as some authors suggest? New "myths" or self-understandings on the part of the legal profession? Less emphasis on managerialism and the bottom line? Does lawyers' discontent stem from their background or the existing traits (such as compulsiveness) that they bring to law school and the profession?[1]

Many other books have addressed law's discontents, including Walter Bennett's *The Lawyer's Myth: Reviving Ideals in the Legal Profession* (2001), Deborah Rhode's *In the Interests of Justice: Reforming the Legal Profession* (2000), Mary Ann Glendon's *A Nation under Lawyers: How the Crisis in Legal Education Is Transforming American Society* (1994), and Anthony Kronman's *The Lost Lawyer: Failing Ideals of the Legal Profession* (1993), each offering a different interpretation of the problem.

Bennett searches for a new mythology that will enable legal education to join law with moral training and thus overcome ethical disquiet—the lawyer's secret fear that much of what he or she does is immoral.[2] For Rhode, lawyers' discontents stem from the pursuit of money and power—commodities that the average lawyer does not command in his or her own right but manages for others—at the expense of other values, including the public interest.[3] For Glendon, the problem is rapid social change leading to loss of faith in the common law heritage, coupled with "romantic judging" that has replaced respect for the rule of law. She also places the blame on realists such as Oliver Wendell Holmes for disdaining reason, morality, and tradition and replacing them with a pervasive cynicism.[4] (Many members of the public, too, believe that lack of ethics is the problem.) These tendencies feed a growing commercialization of law and a rise in litigation.[5] For his part, Kronman echoes Glendon's charge that postmodern teaching leaves students unmoored and uninspired. He also deplores the recent trend to managerialism in judging and the concomitant decline of the lawyer-statesman and wise counselor, especially in the large firm.[6] His solution as well entails a turn to the past in an effort to recapture classical ideals of wisdom and prudential judgment.

Formalism and Unhappiness

We believe that each of these impressive works captures only part of the situation, and that as the story of Archibald MacLeish and Ezra Pound shows, lawyers' unhappiness contains both a conceptual and a phenomenological dimension. The two are linked, the conceptual one having to do with the fetters that lawyers and judges place on their own method, the phenomenological one with the felt experiences of practicing under those limitations and in workplaces designed with them in mind. For us, MacLeish's predicament, like that of many lawyers today, has roots in an approach to law and legal practice known as legal formalism. In law, formalism is connected to the rule of precedent and conservative judging. In legal education, it manifests itself in the teaching of rules and doctrines at the expense of social analysis. Formalism exalts internal values, such as ironclad consistency over ambiguity, sterile rationality over multifarious interpretations, rigid rules over social context and competing perspectives.[7] In legal practice, it appears in the form of narrow specialization, hierarchical organization of the law firm, the relentless pursuit of billable hours, and elephantine briefs addressing every conceivable eventuality and line of authority.

Legal formalism finds counterparts in other disciplines, although we do not explore them in any great detail.[8] For example, in history it directs inquiry to wars and the careers and accomplishments of great men to the exclusion of the roles of immigrants, women, laborers, and ordinary people. In literary interpretation, it focuses attention on the text and its meaning, rather than on the author and the social setting in which the work was written. Formalism limits the intellectual independence of broadly educated lawyers, caring, patient-centered physicians impatient with HMO rules, and scholars in a host of fields who wish to think beyond disciplinary boundaries.[9] Formalism is the intellectual counterpart of the industrialization juggernaut that D. H. Lawrence deplored. Destroying the rhythm of life and the English countryside he loved, smokestacks, coal chutes, and damp mines cast a pall over the work and life of the English laborer.[10] Formalism, if carried to an excess, can numb, setting us up for takeovers, silent or overt, by bureaucracies, large corporations, or the state.[11]

Formalism does confer advantages. It reduces to routine that which should be routine.[12] It enables the rapid delivery of a product, such as the application of syllogistic reasoning to recurring situations falling under well-known rules.[13] But if taken to an extreme, it can draw all spirit out of work, robbing it of richness, detail, juice, and anything else that might render it sustaining. Even MacLeish, in midlife, deplored the "substitution [of] . . . the methods of scientific inquiry, carried over into the humanities," which he believed "destroyed the loyalties and habits of the mind" of a generation of professionals and scholars.[14] A competing approach, known as critical theory, entered law with the path-breaking work of the legal realists in the early years of the twentieth century. Scholars such as Karl Llewellyn, Lon Fuller, and Jerome Frank wrote that judicial reasoning was rarely determinate, that many cases allowed more than one right answer and that in selecting among the many available alternatives, courts and lawyers should be free to consider multiple sources of knowledge.[15] Today, we take those principles of legal thinking for granted, but at the time they were truly revolutionary. The unhappy MacLeish in his Harvard Law School career narrowly missed the full flowering of legal realism[16]—

just as lawyers who enter law today are beginning to suffer from its gradual erosion. MacLeish, however, was doubly cursed, for in his undergraduate literary studies he received training in the ornate formalism of Victorian writing.[17] This is what the imagist Pound, who wielded words like a scalpel, detested in the younger man's writing.[18]

The succeeding sections survey the various types of unhappiness that lawyers suffer and the pathologies they exhibit. In doing so, they make a case, on both theoretical and psychological grounds, for critical theory as an antidote to the dissatisfaction gripping legal practice and education today (and maybe other professions as well).[19] Law tends to attract generalists—broadly educated young men and women with backgrounds in literature and the humanities who wish to devote their lives to the betterment of society. While not every law student is thus motivated, many are; these are the ones who most find law narrow, technical, and dull. After a semester or two, they lose interest in the dance of doctrine and Socratic games, and tune out.

Later, when they enter practice, they find big-firm life little better.[20] Even those who pursue public-interest careers find their longings unsatisfied. They encounter harried, time-pressured judges and court administrators, racist prosecutors and juries. They lose cases they know they should have won, win cases they realize they should have lost. Their clients lie to them all the time. After a few years, disillusion and burnout set in. Might it be that developing their own critique of social institutions and the role of law while in law school could stave off professional disappointment for these highly principled, broadly educated young humanist-lawyers, armoring them against psychological distress and professional burnout down the line?

Even the practitioner who works in a large law firm might gain from the realist approach. It can help the pressured young lawyer to understand the source of those pressures and whence they emanate.[21] He or she may then either make peace with those pressures, or develop means to counter them. Finally, the lawyer with a grounding in critical theory can assist the profession in advancing all the objectives that Kronman, Glendon, Rhode, and Bennett highlight, while attending to the neglected theoretical and social dimensions of legal work. Our counter-formalist analysis might prove useful as well to physicians complaining of bureaucratized, by-the-numbers medicine, academics laboring under regimes of excessive ac-countability, and other professionals squeezed by routinization, specializa-tion, and loss of opportunities to display creativity and imagination on the job.

Now, it is time to look at an unhappy profession in greater detail. What do ABA studies and reports by journalists, sociologists, and lawyers them-selves say about the hedonic level of lawyers' lives? What do we know about billable hours, inadequate opportunities for pro bono work, career pressures, addictive behavior such as drinking or drug taking, divorce, and suicide?

Not a Pretty Picture

General surveys reveal a grim picture of an unhappy profession, with a high rate of burnout, job dissatisfaction, divorce, depression, suicide, and drug and alcohol addiction. Job stress runs high, with unrealistic demands for billable hours, narrow specialization, inadequate opportunities for cre-ativity, and intense competition for jobs, clients, and partnerships among the top laments. Many lawyers regret having entered law at all and con-template leaving for another field. Every year, about forty thousand actu-ally do.[22] An entire new industry counsels lawyers who are unhappy with their work.[23] Counselors report that miserable lawyers come to them in droves with almost identical complaints: I feel like a hamster in a cage. I am dejected and depressed. Life is not worth living.[24]

It is not just lawyers who dislike their work or the sort of people they have become. Surveys show that the public feels about lawyers about as fondly as they do toward automobile repossessors or bill collectors, consid-ering them ambulance chasers who feed off the misfortunes of others and are more interested in money than justice.[25] A Gallup Poll rated lawyers below druggists, members of the clergy, doctors, dentists, and college teachers for honesty and integrity and only slightly ahead of professional admen and used-car salesmen.[26] In a survey of confidence in institutions, law firms rated dead last, behind every branch of government, the military, major companies, Wall Street, the press, colleges and universities, the medical profession, and TV news.[27] A full 72 percent said that society would be better off with fewer lawyers.[28]

Public Perceptions

The public sees lawyers as lacking in compassion, caring, ethics, and honesty, engaged in undignified advertising, and hungry for media attention.[29] Comedians and pundits alike make lawyers the butt of jokes and put-downs; when Vice President Dan Quayle asked rhetorically, in an address to the ABA, whether America needed so many lawyers, a chorus across the land roared back: no.[30]

Among parents who were asked which of eight professions they would encourage their sons and daughters to go into, only 5 percent said law. Ten years earlier, the figure was 12 percent.[31] Among the six lawyers whom people said they admired most, two are fictional and two others dead.[32] Even lawyers said they would be alarmed if their children wanted to go into law.[33] A recent book entitled *The Case against Lawyers* argues that lawyers are amoral and destructive.[34] No other profession seems to have had a comparable book written about it. One author, more charitable than most, thought that the crisis of public confidence and esteem was all a misunderstanding—lawyers and lay people "think and value things differently."[35] Lawyers are indeed competitive and aggressive, needing to dominate and succeed more than most. Not realizing that these traits are inherent in the profession, the public loses sight of their value and perceives lawyers "negatively as cold, dispassionate, uncaring, overly logical, fact-driven, aggressive, competitive, ruthless, and even amoral."[36] Law school tends to intensify these traits, the author concedes. But lawyers have been that way "for several decades [so that] the current crisis appears to be a . . . recent phenomenon."[37]

Job Dissatisfaction Rising,
Especially among Women and Minorities

Job dissatisfaction runs highest among women and minorities.[38] Moreover, it is rising—between 1984 and 1990, according to the American Bar Association's young lawyers section, the proportion of lawyers very satisfied with their jobs fell by a full 20 percent.[39] Only about three lawyers in ten rated themselves in the very satisfied category,[40] and 41 percent of women lawyers rated themselves actively dissatisfied.[41] A study in 1992 found that 72 percent of respondents enjoyed practicing law less now than they did when they began.[42] A poll of alumni of the University of Michigan law school in 1993 found that only 28 percent of those working in law firms of fifty or more attorneys report being satisfied with their careers—down from 53 percent for classes from the late 1970s.[43] Dissatisfaction ran highest with lawyers who are single parents; among parents, women are more likely than men to perceive conflicts between their work and family life.[44]

Lawyers Compared to Other Professionals

Some surveys compare the satisfaction of lawyers with that of the population at large. Surveys show that about six out of seven Americans report being at least moderately satisfied with their jobs, a figure that has remained relatively constant in recent times.[45] Attorneys are much less satisfied. A survey in 2000 found that only 37 percent of lawyers described themselves that way.[46] Other legal workers, including secretaries, clerks, and paralegals, reported much higher levels of satisfaction.[47]

Long Hours and Crushing Workload:
The Billable Hours Trap

Long hours and repetitive tasks headed the list (as they did with the young MacLeish) of what lawyers do not like about their work. An overwhelming majority said that they worked more than forty hours a week. With young lawyers, reports of all-nighters and seventy-hour weeks were common. Half said they worked at least every other weekend.[48] Men were more likely than women to report that they worked more than forty or fifty hours a week in order to generate the 2,200 to 2,500 billable hours a year that their firms expect.[49] The hours spent at work are invariably even greater than that: an attorney cannot bill time spent eating, talking with colleagues, or going to the bathroom. The billable hours requirement at many firms is almost one-third greater than it was only a decade or so ago.[50] Many said that technology increased the sense of pressure: with computers, e-mail, and fax, instant responses are possible, hence expected.[51] As one former practitioner put it, "Ten percent of a lawyer's soul dies for every 100 billable hours worked in excess of 1500 per year."[52]

Nor do attorneys willingly accept such crushing workloads because they love the work or in return for a high salary. In 2000 a survey showed that 45 percent of associates would give up $30,000 to $50,000 of their salaries to cut their billable hour requirement by five hundred a year (that is, by about 9.6 a week).[53] Still, like lemmings drawn to the sea, law students continue to seek work at those law firms ranking highest in number of billable hours required. The two prestigious firms with the highest billable hours requirement out of 165 law firms in one survey were also those that law students cited as most appealing.[54] Perhaps one reason why students are drawn to these firms is the crushing amount of educational debt that many of them incur. What one writer called "the indentured generation" owes an average of $84,400 on graduation, a level that prevents two-thirds of graduates from even considering jobs in government or public service.[55]

Professor Mary Ann Glendon of Harvard Law School, who lays the blame for lawyerly misery on a lack of ethical training, sees a connection between billable hours and the profession's crisis. Hourly billing, which did not become widespread until the 1950s, encourages lawyers to hand in an inordinate number of hours at the end of a workday.[56] Since no human being can bill that many hours and still lead a normal life, lawyers lie. "It fosters an ethically corrosive atmosphere," Glendon says, "where everyone fudges their time sheets. If you are dishonest on your time sheets, it builds an atmosphere of cutting corners on 'little stuff' that breeds a sort of moral myopia."[57] Chief Justice Rehnquist may have been close to the mark when he said that the system of billable hours treats the associate "very much as a manufacturer would treat a purchaser of 100 tons of scrap metal: If you use anything less than the 100 tons that you paid for, you simply are not running an efficient business."[58]

Describing his experience in a large firm in Minneapolis, the author of a much-cited law review article writes: "We were working constantly. . . . [and] constantly feeling guilty about hardships we were imposing on each other and our children. The life we were leading was not the [one] we envisioned."[59] At the time he worked for the firm, it had won a judgment of more than $5 billion for the plaintiffs in the Exxon Valdez oil spill litigation. If the judgment were affirmed, the partners stood to become very wealthy. Pressure on some of the associates was so intense that some "decided to leave . . . and to leave the Exxon money behind. We decided to give up a ton of money in return for work that was more enjoyable and less stressful."[60]

Time as a measure of value, as one writer put it, has its critics. But can the profession set aside the measure if it is part of a structure of thought and a culture that emphasizes form, that divides up cases into tiny parts, and treats well-trained professionals as cogs in a machine?[61] And can a lawyer who adjusts to a law office organized that way (and who trains at a law school that teaches law in machine-like terms) enjoy a normal, happy life outside the firm? "What view of the shape of a lawyer's life, of a human life, is fostered by that worldview?" one lawyer asks.[62] "The habit of treating time as a commodity with a price tag can seep into other aspects of lawyers' lives,"[63] including their nonwork relationships. Time spent with friends and family is treated in financial terms, in light of "trade-offs" and opportunity costs.[64]

Repetitious, Cookie-Cutter Work

Also high on the list of grounds for dissatisfaction was the repetitious, boring nature of the work. In 1984, according to one survey, 30 percent of respondents found their legal work interesting and intellectually challenging; by 1990, only 21 percent found it so.[65] Both the results and the responses seem to reflect the changing nature of lawyers' work. Respondents found that much of the work was a matter of posturing—we would do one thing, and the other side would do another—or mindless discovery of minute facts.[66] "Litigation now is mostly discovery," one associate said. "It's not very interesting."[67] Some laid the blame on overspecialization, with attorneys assigned small portions of the same type of cases, over and over again, "grunt work" that left them feeling underutilized and un-engaged.[68] "You do the same kind of work over and over," one said. "I felt I was getting stagnant."[69] Others called it cookie-cutter work.[70] Except for the partners, few attorneys get a chance to see the big picture, participate in shaping strategy, or even meet the client. In fact, many lawyers have no contact with anyone connected with the case, except for brief interviews of witnesses or while taking discovery and depositions.[71] Such repetitive work, performed under pressure and with high stakes, rewards compulsiveness and compulsive personalities. But psychoanalytic theory shows that reinforcing such traits produces unhappiness and sterile personalities.

Recall how MacLeish, although he admired Harvard Law School, found little more than intellectual patterns, like a beautiful city that only needed excavating. His teachers brooked "no nonsense" about justice.[72] By 1930, only eleven years out of law school, he was a pragmatic anti-doctrinalist who had forsaken formalism and office routine and wanted only to serve the ends of a democratic society.[73] And by the time he was eighty, he wrote that law and poetry had similar goals—the expansion of the human spirit and betterment of society. But he had to leave law school and conventional law practice to come to this realization.

Specialization

In the view of 92 percent of lawyers, the pressure to specialize has greatly increased in recent years.[74] Many worry that they will end up pigeon-holed.[75] One law professor argues that law schools should bow to this increasing specialization by offering fewer general classes in humanistic law, such as jurisprudence, and more specialized ones reflecting the new realities of the world of practice.[76] But if specialization is a source of lawyers' troubles, adjusting them to the unsatisfying role they will fill is hardly a long-term solution.

Large, Impersonal Offices and Firms

Many lawyers commented on the impersonal quality of working in large, factory-like firms and agencies, some with over a thousand lawyers. In such settings, it is hard to get to know the other attorneys or even understand the chain of command.[77] The big paycheck does not compensate for the long hours, sterile atmosphere, and tedious detail. The atmosphere is not warm or personal; it is solitary, with many hours passed in the library.[78] According to one critic: "The law firm work environment which our most able law students enter will diminish them in significant ways."[79]

Lawyers in the largest, most élite law firms were the best paid, but among the most unhappy. Many daydreamed about leaving—or actually left.[80] A leading commentator flatly warned students interested in happiness to avoid large firms, where one risks becoming a high-paid drone.[81]

Lack of Stimulation

One state survey found that the vast majority of lawyers—94.5 percent—are least satisfied with the challenge and stimulation of their jobs.[82] One firm is no better than another, according to one lawyer in New York. "It is the [very] practice of corporate law that has become boring and unfulfilling."[83] Lawyers in new or rapidly developing fields were less likely than ones in established fields to find the work dull.[84]

Lawyers wish they had more enjoyable, varied work. According to a recent survey, this is intensely important to them. And they seek it: 87 percent of mid-level attorneys said they factored their level of interest in what they do into the decision to stay or flee.[85] No wonder—survey after survey shows that years of drudgery and routine take their toll.

Poor Collegial Relations and Hierarchy in the Workplace

Other recurring complaints centered on collegial relations and the hierarchical nature of the law firm or office. Asked what they dislike in their colleagues, more than half chose "obnoxiousness," and almost as many "conceit" or "inflexibility."[86] Many thought that incivility and hardball tactics were growing in the profession generally.[87]

Unfortunately, lawyers who find their work intellectually unchallenging, their offices hierarchical and full of stress, and their colleagues dull and inflexible find little refuge in family life either. An alumni survey by the University of Michigan cited an inability to balance the demands of work and family life as one of the greatest sources of stress.[88] Nearly two-thirds of respondents said that the people they lived with had to cope with the lawyer's excessive hours and work-related stress;[89] one survey reported that barely a majority of lawyers were satisfied with the balance between their work and nonwork lives.[90] One-third expressed active dissatisfaction with it.[91]

Competitiveness

A lawyer's life, especially in large firms, is an unending series of challenges. Competition for a coveted partnership is keen; many will fall by the wayside.[92] The base of the "pyramid" at the top firms keeps getting broader, with an ever-widening stable of associates, most of whom will never become partner, generating billable hours and profits for the partners, who live like kings.[93] Impossible work expectations pressure young associates to see who can come closest to meeting them. Lawyers, of course, must win to earn their fees, adding another layer of competition to daily life.[94] Lawyers compete with each other for partnership, with the attorney on the other side for concessions, favorable rulings, and court victories, and with other firms for business and clients.[95] Associates are often assigned cases that rankle their consciences, on behalf of clients they find abhorrent. They must still muster the instinct to win. Rarely can they "chill out," in the words of one ABA writer,[96] or relax with someone at work. Even relations with one's colleagues can turn cutthroat.[97] The civility of the legal profession, which once allowed attorneys to forgive each other's minor mistakes, accommodate each other's schedules, and treat each other with respect, has largely passed into history.[98]

Just a Business

Many lawyers lament that law seems more a business than a profession. Old-time lawyers have said that the profession is becoming more mercenary and less of a learned calling that gives practitioners time to think.[99] Lawyers know that their salaries, and their firm's ability to grow and hire, depend on bringing in new clients, and on milking all they can out of current ones.[100] Even established lawyers who do not generate enough business for the firm are pushed out.[101] Costs need to be cut; the firm offers fewer perks year after year.[102] During hard times, some firms even fire lawyers; everyone's job is insecure.[103]

Everything one does is judged by the bottom line. One much-cited commentator posits that focus on the extrinsic goods of money and status has left the intrinsic goods of law practice—satisfaction in a job well done, a client helped—in the shadows.[104] These intrinsic goods now receive recognition only insofar as they assist the firm by burnishing its image with potential clients and increasing its profits. (Note that the public shares this view of lawyers, believing that they only act out of mercenary motives.)[105] A leading article on lawyers' satisfaction was entitled "Soul for Sale." Of course, the pressure to make money generates pressure to win, since winners make money and losers do not. Even partners feel the pressure to bill a large number of hours.[106]

The pressure of billable hours is said to have caused the death of mentoring.[107] Time that any attorney spends mentoring another or being mentored is nonbillable. Time pressure and billable hours, in turn, generate a second pressure: from clients.[108] Clients paying high legal bills want results, and want them quickly. If unsatisfied with one firm, they find another. Attorneys working on a case know that the firm wants them to bill more; the clients, less.[109] No wonder many feel caught in a double bind. Even MacLeish, writing in *Fortune* seventy years ago, noted that the best lawyers displayed a shopkeeper's mentality.[110]

Lack of Opportunities for Pro Bono Work and Public Service

Many lawyers, especially minorities, women, and the young, complain that their jobs do not allow them sufficient time or opportunity to apply their skills for the betterment of society. In one survey, 58 percent of all lawyers said they would like to have more time for pro bono work— service on behalf of clients such as death row prisoners, children, cultural organizations, or poor people who cannot afford the firm's ordinary rates.[111] One respondent said that many of her peers who planned to devote a portion of their energies to projects such as these had essentially given up. "You don't hear much about it any more. Who wants to pick up a pro bono project when you're working till ten every night on commercial matters?"[112] A state bar president attributed attorneys' decreasing pro bono work to the pressure for billable hours. Few firms give the same weight to pro bono hours as they do to the ordinary kind.[113] "I am fairly active (in) pro bono work," one lawyer said, "but I do it to my own detriment."[114] According to another lawyer, who chairs an ABA advisory committee, many poor clients are not even aware that free legal help is available.[115] Evidently, the bar is doing a poor job of getting the word out— perhaps because many lawyers simply lack the time to perform unpaid work.[116]

Poor Public Image

The public, as mentioned earlier, has a poor impression of lawyers as greedy, uncaring individuals who love conflict and will do anything to drive up the cost of a transaction.[117] Lawyers never call back, and when they do they seem always in a hurry. They give the impression of being so value-neutral that they could just as easily be arguing the other side. In one poll, more than half of respondents did not find lawyers caring or compassionate.[118] Barely one in five said that the phrase "honest and ethical" described lawyers. Whether true or not, these perceptions take their toll: 88 percent of lawyers in one state poll felt that the public's view of them was becoming less positive.[119] Many say they are sometimes embarrassed to admit that law is their profession.[120] Image aside, clients come to legal offices when they have problems. They are in trouble, scared, preoccupied, and at their worst. Lawyers see people in this frame of mind all the time.[121]

Entertaining Doubts, Thinking of Leaving

Nearly half of respondents in one national survey were so dissatisfied with their work that they were thinking of leaving the profession.[122] One might think that the proportion of those considering that option would be higher in large-firm, corporate work, where the pressures to bill hours are highest and the competition for partnership most keen. But lawyers working in government agencies and small firms reported the same incidence of dissatisfaction and thoughts of changing their profession.[123] In one state, 23 percent of attorneys said that they planned to leave the profession before they retired.[124] Many said they would not attend law school if they could live life again, and would not recommend the profession to their children.[125] Three-fourths said they felt fatigued or exhausted by the end of the workday.[126] The happiest lawyers turn out to be those who do not practice law at all. Like the two authors of this book, they teach.[127]

That, then, is the content of lawyers' laments. The careful reader may be struck by how similar these complaints sound to those of the young Mac-Leish decades earlier. MacLeish complained, you may recall, that law is a perfect jungle (hypertechnicality), that it left little time for creative work (workload, billable hours), and that it was deadly dull (routinization). He also found that the practice of law afforded few opportunities for social engagement or creativity.

Although the practice of law has greatly changed since MacLeish's time—not always for the better—one is struck by how much his dissatisfaction mirrors that of present-day attorneys. He studied and practiced during a time when legal formalism—characterized by narrow focus, an emphasis on precedent, and an insistence on law's autonomy and independence from all other forms of knowledge, such as sociology, politics, ethics, and social theory—reigned supreme. After a short interregnum of a few decades in which legal realism, interdisciplinary approaches, and critical thought flourished, today's lawyers labor under such a handicap as well.

Lawyers complain a lot. The skeptical reader may ask: What else is new? Many workers do not like certain things about their jobs. Moreover, lawyers are trained to be critical, to find fault. Perhaps their laments are just blowing off steam, or the fashionable anomie of the rich and powerful unwilling to admit that they have it pretty good. Perhaps our description of MacLeish as an unhappy young man struck the reader that way: a spoiled product of an expensive prep school unwilling to bow to the demands of work and family.

This view requires that we look at the lives of lawyers in a little more detail. What lies behind those unceasing complaints?

5 Lawyers' Lives

Subjectively, then, lawyers seem unhappy. As we have seen, they complain about pressure, workload, monotony, stress, competition, and a public that dislikes them. Still, lawyers are by and large well paid, with enough income to afford doctors, good nutrition, vacations, and therapists to cope with psychological problems. One might reasonably ask: Are the pressures facing lawyers getting the better of them, or are they able to resist them with the formidable resources at their disposal?

It Starts in Law School

Law school is a pressure cooker, with large, tense classes, constant competition, and feedback to the student usually limited to a single exam at the end of the year.[1] Few schools have incorporated the insights of any of the critical schools—or even clinical education—thoroughly into the curriculum. The method of instruction rewards the cocky and the confident. Not surprisingly, many students turn off or stop attending class. Women and minorities, in particular, tend to find law school alienating.[2] Unhappiness was so rife at Harvard Law School recently that the faculty conducted a study aimed at learning why such bright students—the cream of the crop— were so miserable. After a year of research, a consulting firm recommended smaller classes, more interaction with the faculty, and less pressure for grades. Some alumni lamented the changes and felt that the school was coddling students.[3] "Part of the whole mystique of the place was you were on your own and you were not going to get much help and it was tough," said Paul Carrington, now a professor at Duke University Law School. "Unfortunately, the characteristics that make the Harvard Law School what it is don't sell well any more."[4]

Why are law students so unhappy? Undoubtedly, ordinary stress resulting from assignments, papers, and examinations plays a part. But authorities write that law school has a "dark side," its inattention to human needs.[5] Others blame law students for their own problems, writing that law school merely accentuates existing tendencies toward compulsiveness or competitiveness,[6] or say that law students can find law school more fulfilling if they heed the ethical and humanistic side of professional training and refuse to let themselves be caught up in the drive for perfectionism and grades.[7] Another commentator, now the dean at a major law school, suggests that the cure is more pressure, discipline, and routinization, not less. Because that is the way the world of practice is, law schools should prepare students for it.[8]

Law students experience many of the same symptoms—frequent bouts of illness, problems with relationships, weight gain or loss, bitterness and withdrawal, use of chemical crutches including drugs—that their elders in law practice do.[9] Practically every law student agrees that law school made him or her more argumentative. According to one observer, "the cautiousness and critical judgment a student learns to exercise before answering questions remains an element in the classroom through all three years. In its effects, this paralyzes the creative process."[10] Commenting on the difference between a poet and an attorney, the same writer went on to say: "A creative writer or poet is one who perceives things more sharply than the average person. Yet the difference between the creative writer and the attorney is that the creative writer perceives with a total awareness, while the attorney wears blinders."[11] Might not this have accounted for some of the changes that MacLeish saw in himself as he went through law school? Franz Kafka, in a letter to his father, likened his legal education to chewing sawdust that had already been chewed on before by thousands of people.[12]

Law school, intellectually, places students under pressure to believe what is hard to believe. As a top student once told us: "When one attends law school, one experiences daily contradictions—everything framed in [terms of] a series of dichotomies (a far cry from the continuum of reality); the suggestion that there is an objective "right answer" (when judges seem to pick the outcome first, and then craft their legal argument to get to that end); the assertion that all are equal under the law (but then learning that a defendant's race is the number one predictive factor of whether the death penalty will be imposed)—[these] are just a few examples of these contradictions. After being bombarded with these contradictions, is it not surprising that the law student will feel uneasy/ungenuine/conflicted/dis-connected/tortured/confused/betrayed?"

These teachings in law school are asserted as the truth, and anyone who is forced to treat them as such (at least for exam week) may well feel disconnected from reality and any sense of self that he or she once had.[13]

The World of Practice

Once in the world of law practice, the pressures of billable hours, competi-tion for partnership, specialization, repetitious, time-pressured assign-ments, and public scorn take their inevitable toll. Some lawyers adjust to the new demands, but even more suffer some form of breakdown or distress. Unhappiness runs rampant, marital breakup is common, and psy-chological problems are almost twice as frequent among lawyers as among the general population.[14] Lawyers complain that they have no life, no time for exercise or leisure pursuits, and precious little time for family.

No Life, No Time

Although lawyers' laments echo those that one hears everywhere in our fast-paced society, they reach a qualitatively different level. Frazzled, har-ried lawyers snap and snipe at each other and practice dirty tricks—the decline of civility and professionalism is one of the changes most remarked on by older practitioners.[15] Only about 40 percent of lawyers say they derive personal satisfaction from their jobs.[16] But the stress and long hours take their toll outside of work as well. Lawyers arrive home at eight or nine in the evening, exhausted and stressed out.[17] They know they should exercise, eat sensibly, and spend time relaxing with their families. But it takes a while to unwind. Some evenings, reading or proofing remains to be done.[18] And early next morning, the commuter train or subway takes the lawyer to a new day and new challenges. Even the weekend brings little respite. "I have a few hours of relief on Friday night after getting home from the office," one associate reported. "If I have to work over the week-end, this feeling . . . ends almost immediately. Even if I don't have to work, I keep thinking about all the work that's waiting for me to do. On Saturday, I begin to worry about returning to work on Monday. On Sunday, the feeling gets worse, and by Sunday night I'm a basket case. I often don't sleep at all Sunday night."[19] "Work-balance issues are huge," says a manager at a New York office that counsels burnt-out lawyers.[20]

Over the past thirty years the billable hours system has created a "time famine," in which attorneys do not have enough time for personal pursuits or their families.[21] A study by the young lawyers section of the American Bar Association showed that the number of lawyers reporting this affliction increased by nearly one-third between 1984 and 1990 alone.[22] Many said that they had been forced essentially to turn their lives over to their firm.[23] Working the long hours necessary to bill one's yearly quota of 2,200 leaves scant time for anything else in the attorney's life—friends, hobbies, the arts, recreation, fitness.[24] Women attorneys with partners or children are particularly at risk; 74 percent of lawyers working for large firms reported that billable hours had taken a toll on their personal lives.[25] One stated: "I have less time for my friends and family";[26] another, "I have more trouble sustaining an intimate relationship than I used to."[27]

Some firms have recognized these pressures and taken measures, such as short sabbatical leaves and career counseling, to ameliorate them. Most attorneys rate those efforts as poor or ineffectual.[28] Already stressed-out young associates hold on to the hope that one day they may make partner. But they also recognize that achieving that milestone requires, at many firms, an even greater commitment than is necessary for associates. "It's like a pie-eating contest," one said, "where the first prize is all the pie you can eat."[29] Many daydream of leaving the law for a different calling, such as operating a small farm or acting in a theater company.[30] A manager of a consulting practice for lawyers in transition reported that he had worked with attorneys who left law for careers in acting, financial planning, inventing children's toys, graduate studies in social work, designing websites, and serving in the Jesuit ministry.[31]

Deterioration of Physical Health

Unrelieved stress combined with hasty meals and lack of exercise takes its toll on physical and mental health, resulting in nervousness, inability to sleep, chest pains, migraine headaches, digestive disorders, and colitis.[32] A study at the University of California of female attorneys found that those who worked more than forty-five hours a week were three times more likely to suffer a miscarriage than those who worked less.[33] A job counselor who works with lawyers said that a career change might be in order "when a lawyer becomes aware of a persistent and gnawing sense that things are not right at work" or experiences dry mouth and skin as he or she approaches the office. The counselor went on to list physical symptoms that are "the first inescapable indication of distress," including "aches and pains [that] migrate through the body, settling in the head, lower back, or stomach," and not eased by painkilling medication.[34] Unfortunately, those symptoms affect many lawyers. As one put it: "I don't have time to take care of myself—go to the gym, sleep, eat healthy." Over half agreed somewhat or strongly with the statement "I feel stressed and fatigued most of the time."[35]

Employing understatement, one authority reported that the lawyers he studied exhibited "physical health . . . not much better than their emotional health"[36] and that attorneys seem to be an unhealthy lot, with a high incidence of depression, appetite loss, trembling hands, ulcers, hypertension, and coronary artery disease. He cautiously declined to say whether this was so because unhealthy people gravitate toward the law or because practicing law makes them unhealthy.[37] As professors who have spent careers teaching and watching vibrant, extroverted young people in the first-year class turn, a few years later, into driven, tense lawyers with facial twitches, graying hair, paunches, and trembling hands, we have less difficulty than this author did in attributing causation to features in legal work environments.

Substance Abuse and Addiction

As we have seen, many lawyers, whether willingly or not, behave as though they were addicted to their work. But others become addicted to alcohol or drugs, which they use to find relief from stress and anxiety. Substance abuse starts in the law schools, where according to a report by an AALS committee in 1994 it is frequent and heavy enough to interfere with the quality of legal education that many students receive. Alcohol abuse, in particular, was higher than for other student groups, including undergraduates, with usage increasing through law school.[38] Nearly one student in eight reported that substance abuse had affected class attendance, and one-third admitted to having driven under the influence of alcohol or drugs during the preceding year.[39] The committee recommended treatment programs patterned after those that the ABA sponsors for impaired lawyers.[40]

Among lawyers, alcohol and chemical abuse runs rampant; indeed, some lawyers' practice consists largely of representing other lawyers under investigation for failure to discharge duties in a diligent, timely manner because of substance abuse.[41] Lawyers as a group are very heavy drinkers, even more than undergraduates, law students, or the population at large.[42] (Throughout much of his life, MacLeish drank copiously, even developing ulcers as a result. Although the evidence is sparse, it seems that his drinking may have begun during his stress-filled years in practice.)[43] One state study reported that over one-sixth of lawyers drank three to five alcoholic beverages every day.[44] Another found that 18 percent of lawyers were problem drinkers, a rate nearly double that of the population at large.[45] Other studies say that the frequency of substance abuse may range up to thirty times higher than that of the population at large.[46] One revealed that over one-fourth of attorneys had used cocaine, a rate much higher than that of the general population.[47] Yet another study revealed that as many as 70 percent of lawyers were likely to experience problems with alcohol during their careers.[48] One psychologist whose practice consists largely of lawyers linked their heavy alcohol use to stress, overwork, depression, and what he called "justifiable paranoia"—the sense that everyone is out to get you and that the public regards you with disdain.[49] Substance abuse was a factor in 80 percent of disciplinary complaints.[50] Most state bar associations operate formal programs to assist lawyers who are found to be impaired because of alcohol or chemical dependency.[51] As one writer put it, "Practicing law while coping with addiction is a high-wire act. One misstep can send a lawyer's professional and personal life tumbling."[52]

Divorce and Family Problems

Marriage or living with a long-term partner is a significant mitigator of stress and a source of happiness.[53] And couples with high marital satisfaction show lower levels of psychological distress of all kinds than ones who are less satisfied with their relationship.[54] Yet lawyers divorce often; women lawyers, at a rate twice that of physicians and one-third higher than that of teachers.[55] And after a divorce, women lawyers tend not to re-marry.[56] But in most firms women who ask for part-time or flex-time work are stigmatized as opting for the "mommy track" and risk jeopardiz-ing their chances at partnership.[57]

Just as marriage is good for people, divorce can be bad.[58] Divorced people die younger and suffer from cancer and heart, digestive, respiratory, and infectious disorders more often than those who live with a marital partner. And the divorced suffer a much increased incidence of psycholog-ical problems, ranging from depression to schizophrenia and suicide.[59] The divorce rate of lawyers, particularly women, is higher than for all other professionals, even ones in high-stress lines of work like medicine.[60] Even in law school, partners note that the student becomes more argumentative and less easygoing. Casual conversations turn into cross-examinations.[61]

The high incidence of marital breakup and unhappiness among lawyers should come as no surprise. The pressure, lack of time, anxiety, and depres-sion that many lawyers feel are scarcely calculated to produce a happy, caring, egalitarian mate. MacLeish's son, for example, reports that his father was a cold, distant parent who had a number of extramarital affairs. This pattern may simply have been picked up from the MacLeishes' fash-ionable friends. But might it not also have been set during Archie's years as a young lawyer, when his children were small?[62]

Depression and Suicide

Among the many forms of psychological distress that lawyers suffer, de-pression ranks near the top (along with anxiety).[63] Indeed, out of 105 occupations, lawyers came in first in depression,[64] with a rate 3.6 times higher than that of nonlawyers who shared key sociodemographic traits.[65] A disproportionate number of lawyers also commit suicide.[66] Depression increases sharply during law school. A study of law students in one state showed that on entering law school, they suffer from depression at a rate comparable to that of the general population. One semester later, 32 per-cent were seriously depressed, and by the end of the fifth semester, 40 percent were.[67] Male lawyers were two and a half times more likely to suffer depression than the average man. One state study found that 37 percent of all lawyers reported being depressed and 42 percent lonely during the previous few weeks. Almost a quarter of those responding (24 percent) reported symptoms of depression, such as loss of appetite, insomnia, suicidal thoughts, or extreme lethargy at least three times a month during the previous year.[68] Feelings of isolation and loneliness are extremely common. One psychotherapist who treats lawyers reports that many of his patients, when asked what they do, for example at a social gathering, will not admit that they are lawyers.[69]

Lawyers entertain suicidal thoughts far more often than nonlawyers of comparable background—perhaps twice as often.[70] They are also much more likely to seriously contemplate suicide.[71] One state study found that 11 percent of lawyers had considered suicide at least once a month during the past year.[72]

Burnout and Dropout

It was her seventh month at the firm, and already Georgina was having doubts about her choice of profession. A friend who had gone to graduate school when Georgina started law school and was now a community college professor had sent her an article about lawyers dropping out.[73] On it, she had attached a yellow stick-on with the words, "Et, tu?" scribbled on it and the friend's phone number. Georgina had reread it just this morning on the train to work. The article described a young lawyer in one of the very firms that had offered Georgina a job, who had just dropped out to start a round-the-world trip. One of the quotes from him stuck in her mind: "I looked up the line and saw a lot of partners who didn't seem all that happy, either. I decided I didn't want it. I just didn't want to go back to the pressure cooker."[74] The lawyer, who had been a high-powered associate at one of the world's biggest firms and was planning to sail in Hawaii, bum from Europe to India, and backpack in New Zealand before looking for an entirely new line of work, said that a few of his colleagues at the firm told him he was throwing his life away. But most told him that they wished they could run away, too.[75]

Lawyers talk constantly about being burned out. The article that Georgina's friend sent her reported that large firms across the country are aware of the discontent among their young associates, over half of whom, according to an ABA survey, were dissatisfied with their work.[76] Many leave, even before arranging a replacement job.[77] Although burnout corresponds to no accepted psychological category or syndrome, it seems to carry a well-defined meaning among lawyers—a state, produced by stress, over-work, and mental and physical exhaustion, in which the lawyer can barely manage to face the day. Life is joyless, one incessant demand after another. The lawyer's attitude toward his or her job is a mixture of cynicism and dread. He or she harbors thoughts of fleeing, of giving notice, of finding a less stressful practice or leaving for an entirely different kind of work. Burnout seems to include many of the pathologies we have discussed: anxiety, depression, job dissatisfaction, inadequate time for one's family and interests, and a sense that the future holds nothing but more of the same. A study by the RAND Corporation of lawyers in California showed that this condition describes a very large proportion of them. Only half said that if they had to do it again, they would become lawyers.[78] A study of lawyers in North Carolina showed that almost half hoped to leave law before the end of their careers; 40 percent would not encourage their children to follow in their footsteps.[79] A poll conducted by *California Lawyer* showed that 70 percent of respondents would choose a new career if they had the opportunity.[80] Intense job dissatisfaction afflicts lawyers in all positions—associates, partners, lawyers in firms small and large.[81] A survey of young attorneys in the early months and years of practice showed that 27 percent were already somewhat or very dissatisfied with their chosen profession. Almost one-third said they were strongly inclined to leave their current positions within the next two years, and another third said they might consider doing so.[82]

Lawyers do not merely think and talk about dropping out. Many do, especially leaving large-firm practice for the small-firm variety.[83] Out-placement counselors who work with lawyers report helping them find jobs as diverse as actor, financial consultant, and social worker.[84] The ranks of ex-lawyers in one city in Florida included a bookstore owner, a profes-sional triathlete, a TV weather forecaster, a website entrepreneur, and a half-dozen members of the clergy.[85] One dropout became a newspaper reporter; one of the areas he writes about is lawyers who drop out![86] Other dropouts do law work, but only part time.[87] When one of the young defectors about whom Georgina read returned from his travels, he joined a committee on part-time law practice. "Two years ago," he said, "there were 40 people on that committee. Now there are 50." He added, "You know, I walked away from a hell of a lot of money. But I can live on a lower salary. And I can live without the pressure cooker."[88] A partner at a major firm predicted that the top starting salaries in 2020 will be about $270,000, but added: "don't get too excited. If things go as predicted, there won't be any time to spend that money on play, as the profession is likely to become an intensified version of its current workaholic self."[89]

Are Things Better in Small Firms?

Practice in a small firm is less impersonal than in a three-hundred-lawyer megafirm[90] and in some cases less hierarchical.[91] Competition for partnerships may be less keen as well, if only because the stakes are lower[92] and the pressure to generate billable hours correspondingly less.[93] Are lawyers in small firms happier than their large-firm counterparts? The evidence is split; some surveys indicate that they are[94]—primarily because of the greater autonomy that small-firm practice affords[95]—while others suggest the opposite.[96]

Much small-firm work is repetitive—family law, wills, and misdemeanor defense, for example—and some is decidedly grubby and poorly paid.[97] And if, as we suspect, formalism (both as a habit of mind and as a way of organizing work) is a major contributor to professional discontent, practicing formalism in small groups should be little better than doing so in large ones. It might be easier for a group of determined lawyers to break free from formalism's constraints in a small firm than in a large one with an established culture. Still, the hope that "small is better" seems to us largely a vain one.

6 Other Professions

MEDICINE

Lawyers are not the only unhappy profession; nationwide, dissatisfaction among doctors is widespread and growing.[1] Just as university professors complain of excessive accountability and erosion of tenure, physicians complain with particular vehemence about managed healthcare and a system of rules that robs them of time, autonomy, and even self-respect. One study showed that 83 percent of physicians were discontented with this aspect of their professional lives.[2] While managed care and HMO rules are intended to control costs by holding doctors accountable for their decisions, for example their referral of a patient to a specialist, they also limit the time that physicians may spend with patients and undercut their ability to provide what the doctors may consider proper care. The rules impose a huge burden of paperwork on doctors, press them to be hyperefficient, and insert a level of oversight between the doctor and his or her patients.[3]

Some drop out of medicine entirely, finding it no longer satisfying. Even those who remain believe that the system needs fundamental change.[4] Lack of autonomy ranks high among doctors' sources of unhappiness. (It does, too, with K-12 teachers in a regime of yearly high-stakes testing.) One recent survey showed that 94 percent of physicians felt that changes in the way medicine is practiced interfered with their autonomy, while 84 percent felt that this lack of freedom impaired their ability to provide optimal care for patients.[5]

Loss of Autonomy: Cookie-Cutter Medicine

The old world of the practitioner who had complete authority and independence of judgment is gone. "Today physicians practice in groups and answer to benefits managers. Health plans hold doctors accountable for nearly everything they do; they have to justify the treatments they prescribe and the tests they order."[6] A recurring complaint is that a doctor issues a diagnosis, only to have an HMO clerk balk: "We're not paying for that."[7] Some physicians have stopped accepting managed care referrals entirely. "I can't take care of patients less well than I was trained [to do]," said one.[8]

As with lawyers, one ingredient in physicians' dissatisfaction with the current system is time. Doctors spend long hours filling out forms and on the phone getting approvals from insurance companies for treatments that they know will benefit the patient but that the companies do not regard as necessary.[9] A survey in 1997 found that 87 percent of doctors had experienced some form of denial of coverage for treatment that they ordered or wished to carry out.[10] Some doctors try to compensate for the decrease in time permitted them by giving patients printed brochures on their health condition—brochures usually produced by pharmaceutical companies.[11]

Cost Cutting and the Bottom Line: Don't Order That Additional Test!

A related source of frustration for doctors is the increased emphasis on the bottom line. Doctors resent having to practice medicine as if it were a profit-driven business. In words echoed by many lawyers, one physician said, "If I had wanted to be a business person, I would have gone to Harvard Business School."[12] The pressure to cut costs comes from a number of sources: insurance companies, hospital-based health systems, and large physician groups that are overly concerned with profits.[13] According to one, "That grinds you down."[14] Many are reportedly considering leaving medicine for other lines of work.[15] One, who abandoned his practice to work as a handyman, said that although he enjoyed the income and prestige of his former profession, he had become a doctor because he wanted to take care of patients, which managed care made impossible.[16]

As with lawyers, members of the public are starting to worry about whether doctors have their interests at heart: 73 percent of patients in one survey said that bonuses to doctors who cut costs were a bad idea; 66 percent said that such bonuses would lower their confidence in their doctor.[17]

Stress

Physicians find the practice of medicine more stressful than ever. A recent report in *Modern Physician* noted that 81 percent of physicians in a survey taken in 1997 considered burnout a serious problem.[18] Stress has always been a part of the practice of medicine, but long-time physicians believe it is worse today because of pressures to get things done quickly and insurance companies that deny physicians discretion and constantly confront them with quandaries ("If I do this, will I be reimbursed?"). A report in the British journal *Lancet* lays the blame on "a growing disconnect" between on the one hand what the physician is trained and temperamentally inclined to do, and on the other the realities of practice—billable modules, prescribed illness categories and nothing in between.[19] Some reports suggest that stressed-out doctors are giving patients a reduced quality of care.[20]

Stress produces lower satisfaction levels, which in turn are related to intentions to leave medical practice.[21] Peter Moskowitz, a radiologist and former professor at Stanford University medical school, had achieved professional and financial success and seemingly a satisfactory family life despite his eighty-hour workweeks. When his marriage started to unravel and his teenage son began taking drugs, he decided it was time for a change. He left practice for a career of counseling physicians and other health care workers on how to manage stress.[22]

Drug Abuse

Just as lawyers lean on drugs as a crutch, many physicians do as well. The AMA considers drug addiction among physicians a serious problem—even though it may be no more prevalent than among the population at large—because of its ability to impair the care of patients.[23] Like their counterparts in the legal profession, physicians who take drugs report that they do so to cope with the stresses of their work, including having to see many patients in an hour or day.

Specialization

The increased specialization that accompanies managed care has had two immediate effects. It diminishes the role of primary-care physicians—and of dentists as well—who resent being relegated to the role of gatekeepers.[24] And it causes some, specialists and generalists alike, to complain that they are expected to provide care outside their area of expertise. Many worry that patients with complex or multiple conditions will fall between the cracks or become "hot potatoes," with physicians disagreeing over who should bear responsibility for their treatment.[25] Patients complain that no one seems to be responsible for the big picture of their care.[26]

Dehumanization

Early in their medical training—perhaps as soon as their first dissection of a cadaver—physicians acquire a degree of detachment from their patients.[27] But the degree of fragmentation of medical knowledge introduced by managed care increases that detachment and strips physicians of their humanity even more.[28] Physicians "lose the sense that medicine is about caring for people."[29] In Europe, medical training is shifting to address some of these problems, becoming more student-centered and allowing greater feedback from students and participation by patients.[30] In the United States, some medical schools are beginning to teach courses on narrative medicine, literature, listening, and empathy.[31]

Career Change

As mentioned, managed care, specialization, and loss of autonomy are making the practice of medicine less attractive and satisfying than before.[32] Until about 1990, only 1 to 2 percent of physicians changed jobs during a twenty-year career.[33] Since then, the rate of departures has been increasing sharply. Studies have shown that more than 10 percent of the physician workforce changes annually.[34] While some of these changes consist of physicians simply moving to another practice, many are leaving altogether for fields where they can apply their skills in different ways, prompting some commentators to warn of a brain drain in medicine.[35]

Dissatisfied older or mid-career physicians unwilling to bow to the demands of managed care make up a significant portion of those dropping out. Jerome Lockner, a senior internist, explained in a letter to his patients why he was closing his doors after a thirty-year career: "I am just unwilling to get a . . . lobotomy in order to achieve success as a doctor under managed care."[36] He wrote that he refused to bow to a system requiring him to spend hours a day on paperwork, carefully monitor his number of referrals, see more and more patients per unit of time, and turn away the seriously ill.[37] One survey found that Dr. Lockner is far from alone: nearly half of physicians over fifty years old plan to retire or leave their practice within the next three years.[38]

Some physicians take the less radical step of cutting ties to HMOs and insurance companies or seeing only patients who can pay out of pocket.[39] One who did reported that he felt rejuvenated: "I have been un-neutered, restored to my vigorous self. I can finally take care of patients without having to punt the ball all the time."[40]

Disenchantment with the Profession

Disenchantment with the changing structure of medical practice may be behind the recent sharp decline in the number of medical school applications—as much as 26 percent in the last six years.[41] Physicians now in practice say that they are less likely to recommend a medical career to others, even their children.[42] One internist who followed in his father's footsteps, as did his four brothers, advises his only child, a college student majoring in design, against a medical career. "Medicine has changed," he said. "It has become too business-oriented—too much of a numbers game. It's really fun to care for patients and feel needed. But making medicine a business diminishes doctors' enthusiasm for the job. My dad enjoyed his practice enormously. But much of the time I don't enjoy mine, because of the politics and hassles with managed care."[43] In language echoing the lament of many lawyers, 31 percent of doctors said they would not choose the same field if they had the choice to make over again.[44]

7 High-Paid Misery

Just as MacLeish the young lawyer enjoyed money and power but was miserable, many of today's lawyers are so as well. A number of authors have attempted to identify the cause of the profession's troubles in the hopes of finding a solution. In an early section, we considered some of these solutions, ranging from more ethics training (as though lawyers were unhappy because they were bad, or as though adding another level of formalism—*The Model Code of Professional Responsibility*—would solve things), to better myths (as though embracing a more ennobling self-concept would make dreary work more tolerable), to more formalism and less fancy theory (as though buckling down to disagreeable work would make it more palatable).[1] Other writers urge more attention to mentoring[2] (but what if your mentor is miserable, too?), more "lawyer stories" in legal education, or subverting the workplace by telling jokes and subtly mocking its grandiosity.[3] A few, more audaciously, suggest that the workplace itself needs restructuring, with different tracks for lawyers interested in families, and sabbaticals for the stressed-out.[4] Others urge that lawyers take responsibility for their own mental state, by seeking counseling or practicing stress management techniques such as yoga or deep breathing.[5] Only a handful see a link between legal education and method—how lawyers learn to think—on the one hand, and the form of legal practice on the other.[6]

Think Like a Machine? Work Like One

The link is easily stated: if you allow yourself to think of what you do in crabbed terms, you are apt to find yourself working in a crabbed workplace as well. Another way of putting it is that if you allow your repertory of thoughts, ideas, and categories to atrophy you are likely to end up thinking and working in sterile settings. Or, unless you fight against external forces pressing you to reduce what you do to a formula, those forces will make you do it faster, cheaper, and with less room for discretion and autonomy. Work recapitulates thought. This destructive cycle is not necessary; it need not be so.[7] And one can attack it at either end. Dismantling needless regimentation, excessive specialization, and the insane pursuit of more and more billable hours in the workplace frees the mind to consider new ideas. The quest for new ideas may make a suffocating workplace so intolerable that one sets out to change it.

If we are right, then, lawyers and other professionals suffering under regimes of regimentation and stress must insist on the prerogative to think, reason, and be treated as autonomous professionals capable of imagination, discovery, original thought, and dissent. And reformers who wish to humanize legal education and practice would do well to attend to what happens next. When lawyers, doctors, and others are freed from needless regimentation, what will they do with their freedom? What will they think about? How will they practice? Which initiatives will they sponsor?

Of course one must have both discipline and freedom. The raging, out-of-control Pound, whose mind raced from one crackpot theory to another, lacked what MacLeish gained in law school: a rigorous mind and attention to detail. But one needs a balance of rigor and imagination, just as the workplace needs rules, criteria for promotion, and the like as well as the means to recognize and reward innovation. Not to run things into the ground, society needs a sensible mix of adherence to rules and expectations and openness to change.

Perhaps the best way to see how epistemology (how one conceives one's disciplinary norms of truth) and social and labor organization relate to one another is historically. (We deliberately chose the example of Pound and MacLeish for this reason—our hope was that the reader, seeing the phenomenon we describe vividly arising in another era, would be prompted to see how it applies to the present one.)

When MacLeish studied law at Harvard, the school was still under the influence of Langdell, the late-nineteenth-century innovator who taught that law was a science, like physics or chemistry, and that every legal question had one right answer. Students were expected to distill principles of law out of masses of case materials, in the manner of an empirical science. The casebooks were a kind of laboratory, the classroom an opportunity to test what they were learning. This kind of law came about just as the Gilded Age of robber barons and large corporations created a need for an élite corps of lawyers to defend them from injured workers, disappointed consumers, widows, orphans, and people run over by streetcars or maimed by exploding pressure tanks, and to put down rivals and clamoring unions.

This conception of law and legal education also served the needs of the new law schools for legitimacy. But mechanical jurisprudence was not just a useful legitimating tool. It resonated powerfully with the ethos of the time, which was scientific. Darwin had just published *The Origin of Species*. Alexander Graham Bell, Thomas Edison, and Henry Ford had brought inventions and modes of production that brimmed with the promise of even more to come. With science ascendant, the romanticism of the previous period and its love of nature passed into history. Freedom gave way to order and standardization. The railroad tracks had to meet; the crews had to install tracks of the same gauge and width. The parts for every Ford automobile had to fit any other.

The public was thrilled, and the movement acquired an unstoppable momentum. Exhibitions displayed big machines, the bigger the better. The nation was catapulted into becoming an industrial giant.

During the Victorian age, behavior codes set in place rigid social statuses and expectations: parent-child; man-woman; servant-master. The previous period had celebrated freedom and nature. Poets such as Wordsworth, Shelley, and Keats and essayists such as Thoreau glorified nature and the possibilities of the human spirit. The new period repressed emotion—even though, behind the scenes, pornography and other secret vices were flourishing. It was this world into which MacLeish was born. (Pound, too, but he rebelled early, even while in college.)

Today, after a similar period of romanticism and freedom in the 1960s, we are again in an era that celebrates science, order, and discipline. Sputnik sparked fear in America that we were losing our competitive edge. The invention of computers supplied the formative experience of an entire generation, who grew up learning how to perform operations in a specified order and sequence—otherwise the computer would not work.

The practice of billable hours started right around then. At first, the practice was a social good—an attempt to rationalize billing and insure that the attorney was accountable to the client. Billing required early office machines that could process data quickly and accurately; before that, the task had been done by hand. But it became a tyrant, an elevated form of the factory worker's time card developed in the 1920s and 1930s.

Legal reasoning followed suit. The Restatement movement sought to codify and render law uniform during the first period of formalism following *Lochner.* (It is alive today.) Then, legal realism and critical theory sent formalism into temporary retreat, from which it has returned. Computerized legal searching and technology entered law offices in 1985, shortly after the law and economics movement—a new version of formalism— became popular in the law schools.[8] Harry Edwards and the MacCrate Report reminded law schools, in no uncertain terms, that their business was teaching lawyers. And what corporate power wanted from those lawyers was a narrow, technocratic facility at manipulating doctrine, cleverly and endlessly, while of course the billable hours mounted.

During the 1960s, lawyers had more choices than they do today. One could be a people's lawyer, practicing in a storefront co-op with like-minded colleagues, or a revolutionary like Oscar "Zeta" Acosta, or a reformer like Thurgood Marshall and his colleagues at the NAACP. One could defend the poor as a legal services lawyer. The period saw the proliferation of new legal theories such as the warranty of habitability, contracts of adhesion, and the implied warranty of fitness in consumer law. Duncan Kennedy published a bittersweet farewell to that era in his *Legal Education and the Reproduction of Hierarchy.* Self-published and self-distributed, it went through nine printings and sold many thousands of copies.

What We Are Not Saying

We are not saying that freedom and intellectual license are the only, or unalloyed, goods. Pound was free, but a miserable man, a dangerous, un-predictable human being, and a detached father. MacLeish admired him, but not because he was an admirable figure. Rather, MacLeish saw in Pound what MacLeish himself was not, and what he lacked for a balanced, productive life.

Ironically, MacLeish and Pound crossed paths meaningfully only toward the end of two lives that had spun out of control in different ways—Pound's in the direction of license, MacLeish's in the direction of excessive caution and compromise. Today's lawyers—and perhaps physicians and many others as well—are too much like MacLeish. We certainly do not need more of Pound's disorder and indiscipline. But our civilization needs to afford its thinkers, teachers, lawyers, physicians, and ordinary citizens more room to experiment, grow, and breathe.

It needs to do this with *everyone*—not just high-paid professionals. Factory work, for example, contains an irreducible element of routine and repetition. Yet why cannot factory work be made more tolerable, by allowing workers to exchange jobs periodically; providing exercise breaks and opportunities for after-hour sports; permitting workers a voice in how the workplace is structured, and the work done; and offering classes on how the product is made and marketed, and how the machines run?[9]

Formalism and the Creative Impulse:
The Special Case of the Poet

Formalism is not merely an unattractive way of organizing work. Training in it can prove devastating for someone, like MacLeish, with ambitions for poetry. The solipsistic, repetitive, mind-numbing aspects of legal education—not to mention the sheer amount of material to be memorized—can seriously sidetrack any mind interested in art, history, music, or literature. But the competitive aspects of it can be equally corrosive. The professor challenges every word the student says in class; nothing is accepted unless it harmonizes with the teacher's favorite, often undisclosed, interpretation. The young humanist can respond by embracing law school—as MacLeish did at times—and try to become a super-student. Or the student can withdraw into a separate world of internal reservations. "Yes, that is how it is in class, and, I suppose, how it is in practice. But I'm taking time off to read this novel, anyway." The novel becomes an escape from an oppressive reality that will loom again with the next class. His letters show that MacLeish took this approach at times as well, seemingly uncertain which world he would eventually choose as his own.

Poetry and Truth

Poets thrive on sharp perception and details. They struggle to increase awareness of reality and craft language to convey an impression to the reader.[10] The difficulty is that legal formalism hammers reality—in the form, for example, of a client who swindled two hundred widows by selling them worthless stock—into existing doctrines and precedents. It asks whether the case calls up this precedent or that, whether regulation is permissible under this governmental power or the other. Deeming most of the facts of the case irrelevant—including many that would be considered relevant by most citizens—it pronounces this case like some previous one, and not some other. Even when correct within its narrow system, this is always a kind of world-killing exercise—in less polite language, a lie. Constantly reasoning in this fashion erects a barrier between the would-be poet and the world.

Formalism also trains the mind in a number of habits—abstraction rather than detail, similarity rather than difference, generality rather than particularity—that are the opposite of what the poet needs. Poets thrive on acute observation of small details and reflection on what they could mean. Lawyers get paid to overlook details, especially messy ones that argue against their position, and take refuge instead in highly result-oriented abstractions that just happen to make the case come out in their favor.

Judges and Lawyers

Formalist reasoning can take one of two forms—that of the judge and that of the lawyer. Either kind is anathema for an aspiring poet. A lawyer starts from a conclusion and works backward. "My client should win, because . . ." Perhaps the case falls under the 1947 case of X and the 1953 modification of the rule of Y. The lawyer on the other side of course argues the reverse, perhaps by going back further in time to cases that superficially do not look like this one but nevertheless govern a small but important and overlooked aspect of it.

The lawyer, then, starts with a conclusion and works backward, employing the tools of a closed formalist system and arguing that his conclusion follows by logic alone.

The judge works the other way. Singling out a few cases and doctrines from the past over others that could just as plausibly have been applied, the judge reasons forward to reach the present case. Then, as though it were a surprise and not known in advance, the judge announces the decision—this party or that wins.

Both forms of reasoning make up for their deficiencies in time-honored ways. Point out the problems in the lawyer's chain of reasoning—how a case cited could just as easily be seen as falling under some other rule—and the lawyer is apt to respond with lawyerly invective ("How could you believe that?"). Lawyers—even very good ones—become expert at this sort of posturing, bullying, bluffing, and pretended indignation.

On the judge's side, something similar goes on, although the discourse is much more polite. When an appellate court reverses a lower one, because the lower court invoked a group of cases that the higher court was not interested in right now, it will generally observe that the real line of authority is another one—as though skylights that leak, dogs who bite children, and stop signs that are hard to see because of the setting sun came with labels on them ("I am an example of the doctrine of. . . .").

MacLeish, Poetry, and Formalism

The unhappy MacLeish, who for a time tried to be both a poet and a lawyer, struggled against all these forces. At times, he showed an awareness of his predicament, writing, for example, that law was a jungle and that the deeper you go in, the more lies behind you to keep in mind. He also wrote that law offered a kind of fascination but nothing that warmed the spirit. And soon after leaving his practice, he wrote that law and poetry offered very different approaches to reality.

Formalism's effects may explain what Pound and others found irritating about MacLeish's early writing. At times, when writing simply, MacLeish could be a very good poet. But at other times, his writing suffers from indirectness, ornamentation, and allusiveness substituting for the hard work of conveying truth.

Years before legal education took its Langdellian detour, and well before apprenticeship came into being, law was a branch of moral philosophy.[11] A broadly humanistic discipline, it produced not just lawyers but editors of literary magazines, writers, even clerics. A hundred years later, and beginning just before MacLeish entered law school at Harvard, American legal education decisively cast aside any remnants of that tradition in favor of legal formalism. Poetry during that era had been doing much the same, discarding engagement with the world in favor of Victorian sighs and bird trills. Today poetry, like most of the arts, has cast aside the formalist tradition. Law has yet to do so. Legal education teaches, still, through the vehicle of the desiccated appellate case—many stages removed from the courtroom drama and the give-and-take of daily life. The method is Socratic, with a few departures to consider the predictable "broader issues" that an appellate opinion raises. Law practice recapitulates law school, with the same fetters. Only the pay is better. Until law too abandons unnecessary formalism, it will remain an unattractive way to make a living and a burying ground for poets.

Are we saying, then, that all lawyers should be poets? By no means. MacLeish's life is a metaphor for what is starting to go wrong with the world of work. Many lawyers might well be happier if their lives contained more poetry—if they could slow down and read, or even write, a poem sometimes. But thousands more would benefit if their lives contained more leisure, more contemplation, more time to think seriously about what they do, and, even, enjoy it.

The narrative-killing, subdividing, compartmentalizing impulse begins with epistemology and education, with subtle changes in how a profession defines truth and validity. The workplace then changes to follow suit, becoming more rigid with more and more of everything prescribed. The over-regimented lawyer, in turn, finds less opportunity to engage in expressive activity or creative thought, on the job or elsewhere, in a continuing, self-reinforcing cycle whose main beneficiaries are the giant corporations and soulless bureaucracies that need to have such work done.

What will serve as the brake in society's slide toward such a world? Poetry? The human spirit and its drive to express itself through work? The creative impulse? The desire to play? Although each of these is part of the answer, we highlight and name something broader that encompasses all of them—anti-formalism and critical analysis. The riverboat pilot in Mark Twain's *Life on the Mississippi* observed that after a lifetime of navigating boats down that river, he knew intimately every bend, current, rock, and eddy—but in the process had lost the ability, which he originally had, to appreciate the river as a powerful, majestic force full of grandeur. What we do every day, for a living, shapes us and the kind of person we become: what we see, appreciate, tolerate. The old hippie phrase had it: "You are what you eat." That may be true or not. But we certainly are what we do. The Hamlet-like, tortured young MacLeish saw that, and recoiled from the choice, first selecting the one line of work, then the other. Only much later in life did he achieve some balance between formalism and anti-formalism, law and poetry. An unhappy profession today struggles to achieve just such an accommodation, and with no greater success.

Georgina eventually got around to making that list. In fact, she kept it in her desk drawer under lock and key and added to it from time to time. Entitled "My Work Situation and What's Wrong with It," it now occupied nearly two pages of yellow legal-size paper organized under headings such as "Billable Hours," "Pressure," "No Time for Myself," "Boring Work," and "Whatever Happened to That English Major I Used to Be?"

It was eight-thirty one winter evening, the new moon was glaring outside her window, and everyone had gone home except for the word processors and two attorneys in the office next door. After looking around to make sure no one was watching, Georgina took the list out and added a new entry or two. She then looked out the window for a long time.

Squaring her shoulders, she edited the last line of the brief she was writing, shut down her computer, picked up her briefcase, and said to no one in particular: "Tomorrow, I'm going to find time to check out that new bookstore I've been wanting to see."

Notes

PART I Panthers and Pinstripes

1 Other notable poet-lawyers include Wallace Stevens, Edgar Lee Masters, Charles Reznikoff, Sidney Lanier, William Cullen Bryant, James Russell Lowell, Joaquin Miller, and John Godfrey Saxe. See Steven Richman, "Edgar Lee Masters and the Poetics of Legal Realism," 31 *California Western Law Review* 103 (1994); Thomas C. Grey, *The Wallace Stevens Case: Law and the Practice of Poetry* (1991). Masters was Clarence Darrow's law partner.

2 See Case File 58,102, Ezra Loomis Pound, Case Files of Patients, 1855–1958, Records of Medical Records Branch, and Records of St. Elizabeths Hospital (Record Group 418), National Archives, Washington. See Prologue, 20 *Journal of the National Archives* 284 (1988) (announcing the opening of the file).

3 For a comprehensive study of the legal and medical issues of Pound's case, see E. Fuller Torrey, *The Roots of Treason: Ezra Pound and the Secrets of St. Elizabeths* (1984). For other accounts of Pound's life and work, see Humphrey Carpenter, *A Serious Character: The Life of Ezra Pound* (1988); Anne Conover, *Olga Rudge and Ezra Pound* (2001); C. David Heymann, *Ezra Pound: The Last Rower: A Political Profile* (1976); Henry Meacham, *The Caged Panther: Ezra Pound at Saint Elizabeths* (1967); Charles Norman, *The Case of Ezra Pound* (1968); Noel Stock, *The Life of Ezra Pound* (1970); J. J. Wilhelm, *The American Roots of Ezra Pound* (1985), *Ezra Pound in London and Paris, 1908–1925* (1990), and *Ezra Pound: The Tragic Years, 1925–1972* (1994).

4 Pound used the term "the caged panther" to describe himself during his imprisonment by the U.S. Army in Pisa, Italy, and later in St. Elizabeths Hospital. See Ezra Pound, *The Pisan Cantos* (1948), Canto 83 ("But in the caged panther's eyes: Nothing. Nothing that you can do").

1 The Caged Panther

1 Torrey, *supra* note 3, at 18; Meacham, *supra* note 3, at 15; Stock, *supra* note 3, at 5.

2 Heymann, *supra* note 3, at 7–8; Stock, *supra* note 3, at 6, 7.

3 Torrey, *supra* note 3, at 18–23; Stock, *supra* note 3, at 7; Heymann, *supra* note 3, at 6.

4   Torrey, *supra* note 3, at 24. See also Michiko Kakutani, "Pound's Inexorable Mix of Politics and Poetry," *New York Times*, 14 December 1998, § B, p. 4 (Pound, who despised the common man, told *Poetry* magazine in 1914 that the poet is not dependent on him. Instead, humanity is a "rich effluvium . . . the waste and the manure and the soil, and from it grows the tree of the arts . . . This rabble does *not* create the great artist. They are aimless and drifting without him").

5   Heymann, *supra* note 3, at 10.

6   Torrey, *supra* note 3, at 18–41.

7   *Id.* at 28. As a graduate student Pound remained socially inept. An only child, he had grown accustomed to being the center of attention and failed to develop the ability to have casual relationships. Some classmates found him intriguing because of his iconoclasm and colorful manner but were later put off by his self-centeredness. Yet he was capable of loyalty and generosity in friendship, as those who benefited were to acknowledge years later when he was in trouble. See *id.* at 4, 20–22, 26, 29.

8   Stock, *supra* note 3, at 15, 21.

9   *Id.* at 12; Torrey, *supra* note 3, at 25, 30, 32–36. He learned Anglo-Saxon, French, German, Greek, Italian, Latin, Provençal, and Spanish.

10   Stock, *supra* note 3, at 36; Torrey, *supra* note 3, at 37, 38, 40–41. See also Jeffrey Meyers, "Shrinking Pound," *Spectator*, 28 April 1984, 25 (describing Pound's "lifetime of notorious eccentricity").

11   Stock, *supra* note 3, at 53–67; Heymann, *supra* note 3, at 13–16; Torrey, *supra* note 3, at 42. See also Wilhelm, *Ezra Pound in London and Paris*, *supra* note 3, at 5 (reporting that his name began to be mentioned within two months of his arrival). He had visited London briefly three times before. Heymann, *supra* note 3, at 8–9; Stock, *supra* note 3, at 58.

12   The collections were *A Lume Spento* (1908), *A Quinzaine for This Yule* (1908), *Personae* (1909), and *Exultations* (1909).

13   Stock, *supra* note 3, at 70; Torrey, *supra* note 3, at 59–60.

14   Heymann, *supra* note 3, at 17. On the literary scene in the United States before the decade of the 1920s, see Frederick J. Hoffman, *The Twenties: American Writing in the Postwar Decade* (1955), 3–14 (chapter 1: "The Temper of the 1920s," part 1: "The Old Gang and the New"). What Pound didn't want to write about was that spring is pleasant, flowers bloom, a young man's fancy turns to love, men fight and go on voyages. Rather he pursued Beauty and "want[ed] to be free of didactism." Letter to William Carlos Williams (21 October 1908), quoted in Louis Simpson, *Three on the Tower: The Lives and Works of Ezra Pound, T. S. Eliot, and William Carlos Williams* (1975), 5. Speaking on the state of poetry in Britain between 1890 and the time he arrived

there: "a horrible conglomerate compost . . . most of it not even baked, all legato, a doughy mess of third-hand Keats, Wordsworth . . . fourth-hand Elizabethan sonority, blunted, half-melted, lumpy." "Hell," *Literary Essays of Ezra Pound* (1954), 205.

15 Torrey, *supra* note 3, at 54–57.

16 Wilhelm, *Ezra Pound in London and Paris*, *supra* note 3, at 62.

17 E.g., Wilhelm, *Ezra Pound in London and Paris*, *supra* note 3, at 8, 20, 23; Kakutani, *supra* note 8. His brash behavior continued in the Paris period to follow. For example, at one of Gertrude Stein's famous dinner parties, hosted by Amy Lowell at Stein's home on the rue de Fleurus, Pound excitedly tried to explain to the guests the paintings that hung on Stein's wall, gesticulating so wildly that he fell out of her favorite armchair. She resolved never to invite him to her home again. Heymann, *supra* note 3, at 50.

18 Cutting was one of his principal tools. He defended the practice in a letter to MacLeish in 1926: "I find people often can NOT rewrite, they get a thing down, and then get paralysis, and imagine it wont go any other way. . . . [t]here are always forty ways to say ANYTHING and the first one is usually wrong. I don't mean my slashes are definite improvements, merely a suggested possible elimination or change, and a queery as to whether certain words really function." Letter from Ezra Pound to Archibald MacLeish (5 December 1926) (Library of Congress, Manuscript Division, MacLeish File).

19 Heymann, *supra* note 3, at 26–28, 30–31; Stock, *supra* note 3, at 126–27; Torrey, *supra* note 3, at 60–64. Others whom he helped or influenced included Ernest Hemingway, William Carlos Williams, E. E. Cummings, Hart Crane, Marianne Moore, Wyndham Lewis, D. H. Lawrence, Katherine Anne Porter, James Joyce, the French sculptor Henri Gaudier-Brzeska, the Romanian sculptor Constantin Brancusi, and the American composer George Antheil. Torrey, *supra* note 3, at 4–5.

20 Torrey, *supra* note 3, at 48–49. He also broke up several marriages, see, e.g., Wilhelm, *Ezra Pound in London and Paris*, *supra* note 3, at 48, and believed himself a modern troubadour. *Id.* at 48–51.

21 Wilhelm, *Ezra Pound in London and Paris*, *supra* note 3, at 8.

22 *Id.* at 8, 25, 302. See also Heymann, *supra* note 3, at 50.

23 Wilhelm, *Ezra Pound in London and Paris*, *supra* note 3, at 8.

24 *Id.* at 25.

25 *Id.* at 28.

26 Stock, *supra* note 3, at 148–49, 167–69.

27 Scott Donaldson, *Archibald MacLeish: An American Life* (1992), 131. Fenollosa's essay argued that poetry should express the interaction of things and appeal to the emotions. See Archibald MacLeish, Paris Notebook, 1924–25 (February–

March 1924?) (Library of Congress, Manuscript Division, MacLeish File). "This is one of the most important pieces of writing I have ever happened upon."

28 Heymann, *supra* note 3, at 17–19; Stock, *supra* note 3, at 112, 115. This was one feature of Pound's writing that Archibald MacLeish admired but could not emulate. "Public Speech and Private Speech in Poetry," *A Time to Speak: The Selected Prose of Archibald MacLeish* (1941), 59, 93–94.

29 Simpson, *supra* note 18, at 33–34.

30 Wilhelm, *Ezra Pound in London and Paris*, *supra* note 3, at 6.

31 *Id.* at 104.

32 Ezra Pound, *Personae* (1909), 109.

33 *Id.* at 108.

34 *Id.* at 116. The title of the poem is "Ancient Music."

35 Stock, *supra* note 3, at 158–75; Wilhelm, *Ezra Pound in London and Paris*, *supra* note 3, at 200–201.

36 Heymann, *supra* note 3, at 34. For example, in 1915 writing earned him only 42 pounds. See Wilhelm, *Ezra Pound in London and Paris*, *supra* note 3, at 19 (describing his relationship with Mary Sinclair, who fed him and introduced him to her circle of friends). Many of his patrons and admirers were women, see *id.* at 48–51, 53, 122–23, 151–53.

37 Wilhelm, *Ezra Pound in London and Paris*, *supra* note 3, at 56.

38 Torrey, *supra* note 3, at 60. For example, when an obscure poet named Cheever Dunning, who had been a neighbor in Paris, fell ill, Pound gave him money, and even helped to get his work published, with an enthusiastic introduction by Pound himself. He also supported the Italian poet Emmanuele Carnevali when he was sick, sending books and magazines to his hospital bed in Bologna and raising money for his medical bills. A few years later during the Depression, Ford Madox Ford asked if Pound could possibly lend him some money since he and his wife had been without enough to eat; Pound immediately sent $100, having borrowed much of it himself. Carpenter, *supra* note 3, at 441.

39 Torrey, *supra* note 3, at 90, 95, 98–102. Paris was now becoming the new literary capital of Europe.

40 Humphrey Carpenter, *Geniuses Together: American Writers in Paris in the 1920s* (1988), 89.

41 See chapter 2, *infra*.

42 Wilhelm, *Ezra Pound in London and Paris*, *supra* note 3, at 263, 288; Heymann, *supra* note 3, at 50.

43 For example, an essay published in 1903 ("How I Began") explains: "For well over a year now I have been trying to make a poem of a very beautiful thing that befell me in the Paris Underground. I got out of a train at . . . La Concorde

and in the jostle I saw a beautiful face, and then, turning suddenly, another and another, and then a beautiful child's face. All that day I tried to find words for what this made me feel." Pound goes on to explain how he struggled with this experience for nearly a year before producing "In a Station of the Metro." Wilhelm, *Ezra Pound in London and Paris, supra* note 3, at 105.

44 Simpson, *supra* note 18, at 24.

45 Wilhelm, *Ezra Pound in London and Paris, supra* note 3, at 104.

46 Heymann, *supra* note 3, at 30, 51–53; Torrey, *supra* note 3, at 98. Eliot dedicated the work to Pound with the inscription: "For E. P. il miglio fabbro" (the better craftsman).

47 Heymann, *supra* note 3, at 29–30, 51. Pound helped to get Joyce's *Ulysses* published. On another occasion, Joyce needed money for a glaucoma operation. Pound arranged for the sale of two autographed letters by King Ferdinand and Queen Isabella of Spain in his father's collection. Wilhelm, *Ezra Pound in London and Paris, supra* note 3, at 201.

48 He conceived of the Cantos as a long, epic poem, in the manner of Dante's *Divine Comedy*. Wilhelm, *Ezra Pound in London and Paris, supra* note 3, at 182. See also Heymann, *supra* note 3, at 63–67; Stock, *supra* note 3, at 117–18. A 1933 edition of *The Cantos of Ezra Pound* contained testimonies by such luminaries as Ernest Hemingway, Ford Madox Ford, T. S. Eliot, Hugh Walpole, Archibald MacLeish, James Joyce, and others.

49 Ezra Pound, *The Cantos of Ezra Pound* (1970), Canto 37, pp. 181–86 (banks); Canto 45, p. 229 (usury); Canto 35, p. 172, Canto 74, p. 425 (Jews).

50 Torrey, *supra* note 3, at 132; Heymann, *supra* note 3, at 32.

51 Clifford H. Douglas, *Economic Democracy* (1920).

52 Ezra Pound, Book Review, *Little Review*, April 1920, at 39. Pound, one of a group of American intellectuals who flirted with fascism, had shown interest in Guild Socialism in his early London days, Arthur M. Schlesinger Jr., *The Politics of Upheaval* (1960), 72. For others, see note 58 *infra*.

53 Torrey, *supra* note 3, at 132, citing Douglas's theory that people should not be allowed to profiteer from the manipulation of money.

54 Wilhelm, *Ezra Pound: The Tragic Years, supra* note 3, at 56–62; Meacham, *supra* note 3, at 18–19; Torrey, *supra* note 3, at 133. Many other American intellectuals flirted with the Social Credit idea. Years later Archibald MacLeish was to write about this same theory, although in somewhat warier terms. See Archibald MacLeish, "A Preface to Social Credit: The Economic Ideas of C. H. Douglas," *Harvard Graduates' Magazine* 85 (1933). See also Carpenter, *supra* note 3, at 356–59, 466, listing other figures who showed an interest in Douglas's theories, including William Carlos Williams, Herbert Read, and Hilaire Belloc (who liked it because it was potentially anti-Semitic).

55   *Protocols of the Learned Elders of Zion* (V. Marsden ed. and trans., 1978).

56   Torrey, *supra* note 3, at 140. Later he would blame Roosevelt for robbing his ancient father of 40 percent of his pension. Letter from Ezra Pound to Archibald MacLeish (24 March 1932/33) (Library of Congress, Manuscript Division, MacLeish File).

57   *Id.* at 137. See also Schlesinger, *supra* note 56, at 72 (observing that Pound was obsessed with money and monetary reform).

58   Heymann, *supra* note 3, at 54. The Pounds went to Italy to free him from energy-draining protégés and to give him more time to write. While the move did bring him a degree of freedom, it also brought a burdensome and copious correspondence with his now-distant friends. He did, however, find time to contribute to the Italian music scene, taking part in a musical study group in Rapallo. Its members set out to hear as many of Vivaldi's 310 concerti as possible, played by Pound's mistress, Olga Rudge, and other musicians. Pound and Rudge are today considered to have been highly influential in reviving Vivaldi's music, which had by then been almost entirely forgotten. Conover, *supra* note 3, at 124.

59   Tim Redman, *Ezra Pound and Italian Fascism* (1991), 70–71.

60   Wilhelm, *Ezra Pound: The Tragic Years, supra* note 3, at 84–89. Inspired perhaps by Italian educational theory, which was then in a period of ferment, Pound produced *How to Read* (1931), *The ABC of Economics* (1933), *The ABC of Reading* (1934), and *The Guide to Kulchur* (1938). He even imagined himself a self-appointed advisor to universities, with a universal Ezuversity curriculum. Carpenter, *supra* note 3, at 468, 497 (according to Pound, "The ABC has brought many souls to the Lord///They can understand it a damn sight easier than they can Doug."), 518–32. First issued as a series by New York Herald Tribune Books in 1929, *How to Read* had a major impact on American New Criticism and is widely read even today. It marks a transition from Pound the poet to Pound the provocateur and pamphleteer. Redman, *supra* note 63, at 83.

61   See Wilhelm, *Ezra Pound in London and Paris, supra* note 3, at 141–60. Coined by Wyndham Lewis, vorticism holds that creative energy derives from alignments called vortices, and is associated with William Blake and the Greek philosopher Plotinus.

62   See Wilhelm, *Ezra Pound: The Tragic Years, supra* note 3, at 65. The film, *Le Fiamme Nere* [The Black Flames], was never made.

63   Torrey, *supra* note 3, at 135–36. At their meeting, which lasted about a half-hour, Pound gave the leader some poetry and a list of points that Pound wished him to consider, and explained the economic ideas of Major Douglas. Wilhelm, *Ezra Pound: The Tragic Years, supra* note 3, at 70–71. Though Pound offered again to meet with Mussolini to discuss an economic policy for the

fascist government, the invitation was not accepted. Carpenter, *supra* note 3, at 491. Mussolini exerted a considerable attraction on other public figures as well, receiving early praise from Winston Churchill, George Bernard Shaw, John Gunther, and the poet Wallace Stevens, who in a letter to a friend in 1935 said, "I am pro-Mussolini personally." John P. Diggins, *Mussolini and Fascism: The View from America* (1972), 245. The reexamination of Mussolini's ideas continues today. See R. J. B. Bosworth, *Mussolini* (2002).

64 Ezra Pound, *Jefferson and/or Mussolini* (1935), 11–13, 19; Torrey, *supra* note 3, at 136. Interviewed in Belvedere in 1931, Pound compared the two figures, noting that each was interested in land reclamation, "the battle for grain," and economic reform. Redman, *supra* note 63, at 76.

65 *Jefferson and/or Mussolini*, *supra* note 68, at 128.

66 On MacLeish's admiration, see Donaldson, *supra* note 31, at 366–67.

67 Heymann, *supra* note 3, at 69 (referring to thousands of letters); Torrey, *supra* note 3, at 146.

68 Ezra Pound, "Murder by Capital," *Selected Prose, 1909–1965* (William Cookson ed., 1973), 229.

69 Redman, *supra* note 63, at 73.

70 "Murder by Capital," *supra* note 72, at 229.

71 Stock, *supra* note 3, at 15–16; Heymann, *supra* note 3, at 75; Torrey, *supra* note 3, at 68–69. See Ezra Pound, Cantos 74, 76, 79, *Cantos of Ezra Pound*, *supra* note 53, at 425, 452, 484 (anti-black and other racist references).

72 Heymann, *supra* note 3, at 83–86, 88; Torrey, *supra* note 3, at 152; Meacham, *supra* note 3, at 19. Pound's ostensible purpose was to accept an honorary degree, but he hoped to persuade the United States of the error of its ways and avert the Second World War and economic ruin. At least one writer (Ernest Hemingway) believed that receipt of the honorary degree was a high point of his life, and that if he had received more such recognitions his views might not have taken such a strange turn. See Wilhelm, *Ezra Pound: The Tragic Years*, *supra* note 3, at 155.

73 Redman, *supra* note 63, at 98.

74 Archibald MacLeish, "Poetry and the Public World," *Atlantic Monthly*, June 1939, 823. Reprinted in *A Time to Speak: The Selected Prose of Archibald MacLeish* (1941), 81.

75 Donaldson, *supra* note 31, at 289. In an essay written years later, MacLeish was to offer the following explanation of Pound's behavior: "Pound was widely if not deeply read, but his experience of the world was thin. His own country he knew only through the veil of print—largely historical print. Having spent all his adult life abroad, he knew nothing of the crucial American decades from 1914 on: the disillusionment that followed the First World War, the cynicism

and shoddiness of the Twenties, the agony of the Great Depression, the so-cial revolution that followed, the grim decision forced on the country by the rise of Hitler." "The Venetian Grave," *Saturday Review*, 9 February 1974, 26 ("World").

76 Heymann, *supra* note 3, at 84. "You are at war for the duration of Japan's pleasure (Feb. 3, 1942). . . . You are not going to win this war. None of our best minds ever thought you could win it. You have never had a chance in this war (June 28, 1942)." See also Stock, *supra* note 3, at 396 (referring to copies of 125 broadcasts between 7 December 1941 and 25 July 1943, on file in the Library of Congress and National Archives). But see Meyers, "Shrinking Pound," *supra* note 14, referring to 300 broadcasts. In addition to having been poorly received in the United States in 1939, Pound could not afford to relocate there when the war in Europe began since he would have had to come up with transatlantic boat passages of $300 each for his wife, son, father, mother, mistress, and daughter, in addition to his own. Conover, *supra* note 3, at 141–42.

77 Wilhelm, *Ezra Pound: The Tragic Years*, *supra* note 3, at 172; Carpenter, *supra* note 3, at 568, 616–17; Torrey, *supra* note 3, at 149.

78 See Heymann, *supra* note 3, at 117–18 (reprinting Pound's broadcast of 23 April 1942, referring to MacLeish).

79 See chapter 2, *infra*.

80 Archibald MacLeish, *Letters of Archibald MacLeish, 1907–1982* (R. Winnick ed., 1983), 335 (letter to Julien Cornell, 6 December 1945). Uncertainty swirls over how many times the two actually met during this period. MacLeish denies having met Pound before 1939. Yet some biographers believe that he did. Heymann, for example, includes him in a list of writers whom Pound knew in Paris, perhaps basing this assumption on MacLeish's having given the FBI, in 1943, photographs of Pound taken during that period. Heymann, *supra* note 3, at 50, 134. Barry Ahearn, editor of the Ezra Pound–Louis Zukofsky letters, declares, perhaps metaphorically, that MacLeish became acquainted with Pound while living in Paris. *Selected Letters of Ezra Pound and Louis Zukofsky* (Barry Ahearn ed., 1981), 123 (saying that MacLeish "walked out of a Boston law office to sit at the feet of Ezra Pound and T. S. Eliot"). It remains true, however, that MacLeish arrived in Paris in September 1923, only eight months before Pound left; their correspondence does not refer to any face-to-face meetings. And in a letter dated 1927 MacLeish denies having met him, at least to that point, *Letters*, *supra* at 209 (letter to Wyndham Lewis). Indeed, MacLeish wrote to Pound while working on behalf of his release many years later: "I came on some letters you wrote me back in the twenties before we ever met when you were planning EXILE." Letter from Archibald MacLeish to

Ezra Pound (27 August 1957) (Library of Congress, Manuscript Division, MacLeish File).

81 Letter from Ezra Pound to Archibald MacLeish (5 December 1926) (Library of Congress, Manuscript Division, MacLeish File); *id.* (27 January 1927) ("Don't work on some damn thing that I have already chewed over"); *id.* (15 February 1927) ("It is a matter of breaking up the god damned clichés of cadence and idiom"). For MacLeish's responses, see *Letters*, *supra* note 84, at 187–88, 188–89, 191–93, 248–49, 249–50, 263–64. For letters from MacLeish to others concerning Pound's criticism of him, see *id.* at 194–96, 200, 255.

82 Torrey, *supra* note 3, at 167. The court issued two indictments, the second superseding the first. See Heymann, *supra* note 3, at 135, 180–86 (reproducing both indictments charging Pound with broadcasting enemy propaganda, slogans, and manifestos on Rome radio "contrary to his duty of allegiance to the United States").

83 Torrey, *supra* note 3, at 1–8, 176.

84 *Id.* at 177. As though anticipating that he might later plead a defense of insanity, the U.S. Army had Pound examined by three psychiatrists, who pronounced him sane. Meyers, "Shrinking Pound," *supra* note 14. See also Wilhelm, *Ezra Pound: The Tragic Years*, *supra* note 3, at 252–55 (for notes from log book of Lt.-Col. P. V. Holder, who accompanied Pound on the plane trip back to the United States).

85 "Pound Would Call Wallace, MacLeish: Wants Them to Testify at Treason Trial on '39 Talks—Court Will Name Defense Counsel," *New York Times*, 20 November 1945, 11.

86 See Wilhelm, *The American Roots of Ezra Pound*, *supra* note 3, at 81; Wilhelm, *Ezra Pound: The Tragic Years*, *supra* note 3, at 198–200 (describing Pound's attitude toward his broadcasts).

87 See Conrad L. Rushing, " 'Mere Words': The Trial of Ezra Pound," 14 *Critical Inquiry* 111 (autumn 1987); Torrey, *supra* note 3, at 207–18. The doctors' letter to the court is reproduced in Heymann, *supra* note 3, at 189–90; their later testimony in *id.* at 195–202.

88 Norman, *supra* note 3, at 181–83.

89 See Torrey, *supra* note 3, at 227–31. Among the famous, his visitors included Eliot, William Carlos Williams, Archibald MacLeish, Conrad Aiken, Amy Lowell, Marianne Moore, and James Dickey. See Meyers, "Shrinking Pound," *supra* note 14.

90 Torrey, *supra* note 3, at 234–35.

91 *Id.* at 178.

92 *Id.* at 240, 243–44. Pound took his incarceration in relatively good grace, joking about the "bughouse" in which he found himself. See S. Kutler, *The*

American Inquisition: Justice and Injustice in the Cold War (1982), 79–81 (writing that Pound cooperated willingly with his own commitment, perhaps fearing the outcome of a treason trial). He was also highly productive during this period, writing the "Rock Drill" and "Thrones" section of the Cantos, translating two books of Chinese poetry, and publishing more than 130 articles. See Meyers, "Shrinking Pound," *supra* note 14.

93 Torrey, *supra* note 3, at 245–53. Others found the solution perfect as well: Pound's wife Dorothy had herself appointed chair of the Committee for Ezra Pound. She was also his legal representative, with the funds and power to make decisions about his affairs. She and others "relish[ed] the situation of having their own pet genius all tied up in the cage." In particular, she seems to have frustrated at least one effort by Pound's mistress Olga Rudge to get him out. Conover, *supra* note 3, at 179–83. Others made similar efforts from time to time. For example, the American Committee for Cultural Freedom, whose parent group included Bertrand Russell, Reinhold Niebuhr, and Stephen Spender, tried appealing for Pound's release in 1955 but found itself frustrated when Pound's psychiatrist Winfred Overholser refused to cooperate. Carpenter, *supra* note 3, at 817.

2 Pinstripes

1 Scott Donaldson, *Archibald MacLeish: An American Life* (1992); Archibald MacLeish, *Letters of Archibald MacLeish, 1907–1982* (R. Winnick ed., 1983); Archibald MacLeish, *Archibald MacLeish: Reflections* (B. Drabeck and H. Ellis eds., 1986); William MacLeish, *Uphill with Archie: A Son's Journey* (2001). For other biographical information on or by MacLeish, see Signi Falk, *Archibald MacLeish* (1965), Archibald MacLeish, *A Continuing Journey* (1986), and Archibald MacLeish, *Riders on the Earth* (1978).

2 Donaldson, *supra* note 1, at 6–8. She also took a great interest in children's education and the resettlement of immigrants, working for a time at Hull House in Chicago, founded by Jane Addams. *Letters of Archibald MacLeish*, *supra* note 1, at xi–xii. She graduated from Vassar at a time when few women attended college.

3 Donaldson, *supra* note 1, at 17, 20–21. He adored his mother. Her interest in social service may have sparked MacLeish's own. See later sections of this chapter describing MacLeish's discontent with law's narrowness and his law school's lack of commitment to public service.

4 At Hotchkiss he seems not to have been particularly happy, or popular. He struck his classmates as overly serious and solemn. *Uphill with Archie*, *supra* note 1, at 35. See also Donaldson, *supra* note 1, at 32–36; letter from Archibald

MacLeish to his father (21 September 1907) (Library of Congress, Manuscript Division, MacLeish File). "The rooms here are very bare and cold." The boy goes on to request a supplementary allowance to personalize and decorate his room. He is lonely and wants his mother's address.

5 *Archibald MacLeish: Reflections, supra* note 1, at 16. MacLeish served as class poet at Yale and edited the literary magazine. *Letters of Archibald MacLeish, supra* note 1, at xii.

6 As MacLeish put it, he went to Yale during the "blue sweater" era of relaxed upper-class students interested in little more than football, water polo, glee club, conversation, and earning the gentleman's C in their classes. Donaldson, *supra* note 1, at 51–54.

7 *Archibald MacLeish: Reflections, supra* note 1, at 17. An extraordinary, emotional letter to his wife Ada calls his education "dull" (n.d.) (Library of Congress, Manuscript Division, MacLeish File) [hereinafter cited as Ada Letter]. See also letter from Archibald MacLeish to his publisher Robert Linscott dated summer 1930 (internal evidence) (Library of Congress, Manuscript Division, MacLeish File), describing MacLeish's Yale period as unfocused and unsatisfying—"began writing but learned little about it and had little life of my own."

8 See Richard F. Somer, "The Public Man of Letters," *The Proceedings of the Archibald MacLeish Symposium, May 7–8, 1982* (Bernard A. Drabeck et al. eds., 1988), 115.

9 Donaldson, *supra* note 1, at 65–71; see *Letters of Archibald MacLeish, supra* note 1, at xii–xiii.

10 Later he decided to practice law also as a compromise—it was better paid and more secure than the alternatives, writing, teaching, and journalism. Donaldson, *supra* note 1, at 106 (reporting that MacLeish commented in a letter to his mother [dated 18 April 1920]: "It's an uninteresting outlook, isn't it? Most high hopes boil down to that"). See also Ada Letter, *supra* note 7, referring to that decision, as well as his later year of teaching, as compromises. See also Linscott letter, *supra* note 7 ("went to Harvard Law School to avoid going to work").

11 *Archibald MacLeish: Reflections, supra* note 1, at 17.

12 *Uphill with Archie, supra* note 1, at 37.

13 *Letters of Archibald MacLeish, supra* note 1, at 23 (letter to Francis Hyde Bangs dated 25 January 1916).

14 *Id.* at xiii, 26 (letter dated 13 August 1916). He also ended up first in his class and for a time was a member of the law review.

15 *Id.* at 26. The deadening work that MacLeish referred to was a summer job as a tutor.

16 *Id.* at 32–34, 37 (letters dated ca. winter 1917 (?), 22 April 1917).

17   *Id.* at 38–39 (letter to his father dated 5 May 1917) "I have got to go eventually. Something in me stronger than draft-laws makes that imperative." He also found a "certain grim joy" in the thought of enlisting.

18   *Id.* at 42–43 (letter to Francis Hyde Bangs dated 23 December 1917). He saw duty at the front and rose to the rank of captain. Falk, *supra* note 1, at 22. But see Donaldson, *supra* note 1, at 89–94 (reporting that an influential aunt may have got him returned to the United States at a particularly dangerous point in the war, to serve as an instructor at artillery school; back in France, half his former unit was wiped out when the Germans discovered their position in an orchard, which MacLeish had chosen).

19   *Archibald MacLeish: Reflections*, *supra* note 1, at 19. He was an excellent law student, earning the Fay Diploma for the student in his class highest in scholarship and character and with evidence of the greatest promise. *Letters of Archibald MacLeish*, *supra* note 1, at xiii. But it appears that he graduated already despising the law, a system of "rottenly worded rules," and already spending all his free time in bookstores. Donaldson, *supra* note 1, at 100.

20   *Archibald MacLeish: Reflections*, *supra* note 1, at 19; *Letters of Archibald MacLeish*, *supra* note 1, at 48 nn.1–2, 37 n. 8. The collection published while he was at the front was *Tower of Ivory* (1917).

21   Archibald MacLeish, "A Library of Law," 64 *Current Opinion*, February 1918, at 133.

22   *Letters of Archibald MacLeish*, *supra* note 1, at 62–63 (letter dated 30 December 1919). Acheson went on to become secretary of state under President Harry Truman.

23   *Id.* at 66 (letter dated 12 January 1920).

24   *Id.* at 67–70 (letter to his mother dated 5 February 1920).

25   *Id.* at 73 (letter to his mother dated 18 April 1920).

26   *Id.* at 85 (letter to the MacLeish family dated August 1921).

27   *Id.* Later the MacLeishes were less happy together. See Donaldson, *supra* note 1, at 78–82, 135–39, 203, 205–7 (reporting that MacLeish had a number of extramarital affairs). On his role as father to their three children, see chapter 5, *infra*, at note 62 and accompanying text.

28   *Letters of Archibald MacLeish*, *supra* note 1, at 86–87 (letter to Dean Acheson dated 18 September 1921); *Archibald MacLeish: Reflections*, *supra* note 1, at 20.

29   *Letters of Archibald MacLeish*, *supra* note 1, at 96–97 (letters to Dean Acheson dated 8 January 1923, 25 March 1923).

30   *Id.* at 89 (letter to Dean Acheson dated 4 June 1922).

31   Donaldson, *supra* note 1, at 109.

32   *Letters of Archibald MacLeish*, *supra* note 1, at 85 (letter dated ca. August 1921).

33   *Id.* at 86 (letter dated 18 September 1921).

34 *Id.* at 88 (letter dated 22 February 1922).

35 *Archibald MacLeish: Reflections, supra* note 1, at 20–21; MacLeish, *Riders on the Earth, supra* note 1, at 69–75. See also David Barber, "In Search of an 'Image of Mankind': The Public Poetry and Prose of Archibald MacLeish," 29 *American Studies* 31, 36 (fall 1988) (asserting that MacLeish's "growing conviction that to continue practicing law would destroy his poetic goals" was the "primary motivator").

36 *Uphill with Archie, supra* note 1, at 47. Much later, he saw his motivations in a more generous light. In an audiotape of a conversation with Samuel Haro, "Those Paris Years: A Conversation between Archibald MacLeish and Samuel Haro" (1987), he says: "If I hadn't gone when I did, that was about the last possible moment, I was 31 years old in 1923, and if I hadn't gone when I went, I would have continued to be a lawyer. I would have had to be . . . [inaudible] I like the law, you know. The law is a marvelous activity. It's the greatest indoor game on earth and it has serious connections."

37 Donaldson, *supra* note 1, at 125; *Letters of Archibald MacLeish, supra* note 1, at 101 (letter dated 3 September 1923).

38 *Archibald MacLeish: Reflections, supra* note 1, at 25–26.

39 *Id.* at 46.

40 *Letters of Archibald MacLeish, supra* note 1, at 106, 107 n. 3 (letter to his mother dated 14 October 1923).

41 *Id.* at 104 (letter to his mother dated 29 September 1923).

42 *Archibald MacLeish: Reflections, supra* note 1, at 26.

43 *Letters of Archibald MacLeish, supra* note 1, at 117, 169 (letter to his parents dated 26 December 1923; letter to John Peale Bishop dated 8 August 1925).

44 *Archibald MacLeish: Reflections, supra* note 1, at 27.

45 *Letters of Archibald MacLeish, supra* note 1, at 114, 126–27 (letters to his parents dated 8 December 1923, 10 February 1924).

46 Anne Conover, *Olga Rudge and Ezra Pound* (2001), 1–42, 136, 195.

47 MacLeish, *Riders on the Earth, supra* note 1, at 76–77.

48 *Uphill with Archie, supra* note 1, at 50–51; Donaldson, *supra* note 1, at 130–37, 147 (reporting the comment of Sylvia Beach that MacLeish was one of the few American émigrés in Paris who read French literature). See Archibald Mac-Leish, Paris Notebook 1924–25 (Library of Congress, Manuscript Division, MacLeish File) (containing reading notes and poetry drafts).

49 *Uphill with Archie, supra* note 1, at 78; Donaldson, *supra* note 1, at 129–32. See also Ada Letter, *supra* note 7.

50 Donaldson, *supra* note 1, at 134 (citing letter to Choate dated 5 February 1924).

51 Donaldson, *supra* note 1, at 131.

52 *Id.* at 126, 133–34 (Cummings), 144–45 (Hemingway), 152 (Fitzgerald), 174–75 (Joyce). See also Ada Letter, *supra* note 7, listing other writers as well, such as John Peale Bishop, Leon Paul Fargue, Sinclair Lewis, and Wyndham Lewis.

53 Donaldson, *supra* note 1, at 143–44. Gerald, an accomplished painter, was acknowledged by Fernand Léger as providing the "only true American response to cubism." The Murphys possessed charm, grace, beauty, and wealth, and moved easily among artists like Picasso and Stravinsky to whom they introduced the MacLeishes.

54 See Archibald MacLeish, *New Found Land* (1930); MacLeish, *Streets in the Moon* (1926); Langland, "In Our Time for a Long Time," 23 *Massachusetts Review* 663 (1982) (book review) (giving an overview of MacLeish's literary accomplishments).

55 *Letters of Archibald MacLeish, supra* note 1, at 187–89 (letters to Ezra Pound dated 22 November and 3 December 1926); Daniel Aaron, "The Poet as Public Man," *New Republic*, 24 January 1983, 29 (book review).

56 *Letters of Archibald MacLeish, supra* note 1, at 193 (letter to Ezra Pound dated 29 December 1926) ("I can't thank you for what you've done for me. I merely hope to God I'm worth the trouble"); *id.* at 187 (letter to Ezra Pound dated 22 November 1926) ("[I]f I may truth-say without unction of flattery, why I turn to your stuff when my blood changes to sand and the dry grains grate in the heart tubes, is that I do there *hear.* Speech beautifully. Lang-uage"); Aaron, *supra* note 55, at 29.

57 *Letters of Archibald MacLeish, supra* note 1, at 198–200, 207–8 (letters dated 20 February 1927, 18 September 1927). Hemingway, for example, found MacLeish stiff and inhibited, but at times funny. See Ernest Hemingway, *Selected Letters, 1917–1961* (Carlos Baker ed., 1981), 861–62 (letter to Harvey Brett dated 3 July 1956): "The only writer I ever liked, really well . . . Archie MacLeish when he would be funny, and not noble."

58 See Ada Letter, *supra* note 7. He and Ada preferred their own company to watching "fake artists . . . at the Dome" and had little desire to meet "Miss Stein."

59 See MacLeish, Paris Notebook 1924–25, *supra* note 48. A later sonnet about the law proved more successful; indeed Pound, in Rapallo at this time, wanted to include it in an anthology of twentieth-century poetry for the benefit of the "local latins." See letter from Ezra Pound to Archibald MacLeish (24 January 1931) (Library of Congress, Manuscript Division, MacLeish File).

Corporate Entity
The Oklahoma Ligno and Lithograph Co
Of Maine doing business in Delaware Tennessee

Missouri Montana Ohio and Idaho
With a corporate existence distinct from that of the
Secretary Treasurer President Directors or
Minority stockholder being empowered to acquire
As principal agent trustee licensee licensor
Any or all in part or in parts or entire
Etchings impressions engravings engravures prints
Paintings oil-paintings canvases portraits vignettes
Tableaux ceramics relievos insculptures tints
Art-treasures or masterpieces complete or in sets
The Oklahoma Ligno and Lithograph Co
Weeps at a nude by Michael Angelo.

60 Donaldson, *supra* note 1, at 131, 171–73; *Letters of Archibald MacLeish, supra*
    note 1, at 193 (letter dated 29 December 1926).

61 "Poetry and the Public World," *A Time to Speak: The Selected Prose of Archibald
    MacLeish* (1941), 93–94.

62 See "Epistle to the Rapalloan," 33 *Poetry* 184 (January 1929):

Ezra, whom not with eye nor with ear have I ever
(But nevertheless as one by a rhyme-beat, one
By the break of his syllables, one by a slow breath) known,
By doubts that in common between us two deliver
Better your face to me than the photograph,
Which besides they say lies—they say, that is, you were never
The beautiful boy with the sullen mouth, the giver
Of ambiguous apples—Ezra, you that could laugh
When the rest of them followed your hearse in five-years-
ago's mud,
When the rest of them talked of the promise of youth cut off
By a fever, a flush in the cheek, an ironical cough
(That did in truth, they were right enough there, bring blood),
Ezra, I've read your *Sixteen Cantos*:
There's a word for my praise—if there's a rhyme for cantos!

63 *Poetry and the Public World, supra* note 61, at 92.

64 Letter from Ezra Pound to Archibald MacLeish (December (?) 1926) (Library
    of Congress, Manuscript Division, MacLeish File); MacLeish was not to real-
    ize the truth of Pound's criticisms until thirty years later when he reflected on
    his life in a letter to Pound: "I have been cleaning out the attic and I came on

some letters you wrote me in the twenties . . . full of sagacity and good counsel at a time when I needed it badly. . . . I wish I had had sense enough to profit by it then. I might have been a poet by now." Letter from Archibald MacLeish to Ezra Pound (22 August 1957) (Beinecke Library Collection) (custody of Yale University Collection) [hereinafter cited as Pound Letter].

65 Pound Letter (1926), *supra* note 64 (criticizing MacLeish's poem "You, Andrew Marvell").

66 Letter dated 24 November 1926 (Library of Congress, Manuscript Division, MacLeish File).

67 *Letters of Archibald MacLeish, supra* note 1, at 191–93 (letter dated 29 December 1926).

68 "Don't work on some damn thing that I have already chewed over. As it is me you are trying to get cured of, take some god dam sort of thing that I have not used. Arabic, Sanskrit, Pali, Afghan, Georgian, Bulgarian, Danish, wott to HELL. . . . You run down to Berlitz an get six lessons in Arabic." Letter from Ezra Pound to Archibald MacLeish (27 January 1927). See also letter dated 15 February 1927 (suggesting Gaelic).

69 Letter from Ezra Pound to Archibald MacLeish (5 December 1926) (Library of Congress Manuscript Division, MacLeish File).

70 See letter from Pound to Louis Zukofsky (22 December 1931): "If the alternative is [Archibald] MacLeishing for KRRists sake go and do fugues and double cannons and letter puzzles and sequences of pure consonances with no god damn trace of god damn lichercgoor in em AT ALL." Pound and Zukofsky, *Selected Letters of Ezra Pound and Louis Zukofsky* 123 (Barry Ahearn ed., 1981).

71 J. J. Wilhelm, *Ezra Pound: The Tragic Years 1925–1972* (1994), 21.

72 *Id.* at 45. The two kept in touch even through the 1930s, after MacLeish returned to the United States, over publication matters and politics.

73 *Id.* at 325; Mary De Rachewiltz, *Discretions* (1971), 306 ("Then he worried [in Rapallo] that we would not have enough to eat and not enough fuel and Archibald MacLeish sent a check to keep Babbo warm"). Mary De Rachewiltz was Pound's daughter.

74 Their relationship had overtones of sado-masochism. See, e.g., Wilhelm, *Ezra Pound: The Tragic Years, supra* note 71, at 304: "I (MacLeish) don't like to be cursed and I have no intention whatever of holding onto the shitty end of one of your famous correspondences. I know what you think of me and frankly I don't give a goddam. . . . I merely want to be told . . . what I can do in your behalf and then I want a little patience while I try to do it." (Complete letter from MacLeish to Pound dated ca. January 1934 (?) can be found in *Letters of Archibald MacLeish, supra* note 1, at 263.)

75 W. A. Swanberg, *Luce and His Empire* (1972), 83.

76 *Letters of Archibald MacLeish, supra* note 1, at xiv (MacLeish wrote over a hundred articles in the space of eight years); Falk, *supra* note 1, at 50–51.

77 Donaldson, *supra* note 1, at 193–94.

78 Swanberg, *supra* note 75, at 58.

79 *Id.* at 66.

80 *Id.* at 83.

81 Scott Donaldson, *Archibald MacLeish: An American Life* (1992), 187–88 (describing MacLeish's trip to Mexico in preparation for writing the poem), 215–19 (on the reception of the poem).

82 *Id.* at 218.

83 Archibald MacLeish, *Housing America* (1932) (159-page reprint of MacLeish's articles on housing).

84 See *Uphill with Archie, supra* note 1, at 108; Donaldson, *supra* note 1, at 209–10. After leaving *Fortune*, MacLeish published *Land of the Free* (1939), a free-verse poem that accompanied eighty-eight photographs, most from the files of the Farm Security Administration, by Dorothea Lange, Walker Evans, and Ben Shahn depicting poverty across America during the Depression.

85 Donaldson, *supra* note 1, at 232, 237 ("almost joined the Party"), 262 (published two articles in the *New Masses*). In an essay in the *Saturday Review* ("The Poetry of Karl Marx," 17 February 1934), MacLeish rejects Marxism as dated. Social injustice is less a class crime than an inevitable consequence of industrialization. Falk, *supra* note 1, at 70. For more on the Marxist-Humanist debate see Daniel Aaron, *Writers on the Left: Episodes in American Literary Communism* (1961), chapter 8, 231–79.

86 Archibald MacLeish, "In Our Time," *Fortune*, February 1932, 40; Donaldson, *supra* note 1, at 226–27.

87 Donaldson, *supra* note 1, at 228–32. MacLeish's clumsy use of dialect provoked the columnist Michael Gold to accuse him of writing poems "in phony Yiddish dialect to make a joke of the idea that men were brothers." Michael Gold, "Out of the Fascist Unconscious," 75 *New Republic*, 26 July 1933, 295–96.

88 Gold, *supra* note 87.

89 See Falk, *supra* note 1, at 100–117. Even unaligned critics thought that MacLeish's government engagement was corrosive of his style. Robert B. Shaw, Review of *Collected Poems, 1917–1982*, by Archibald MacLeish, 149 *Poetry*, November 1986, 107–9: "His efforts at making poetry perform what he called 'public speech' are mostly unfortunate. His increasing involvement in the public world, so admirable in itself, had regrettable effects upon his style. He was on the staff of *Fortune*, was Librarian of Congress, was even an assistant secretary of state. The poems he wrote from these years suggest that if one associates too closely with journalists and political bureaucrats one's own style

will be corrupted by coarseness, conventionality, pomposity. The damage, once done, was extensive." Robert E. Spiller, Review of *Letters of Archibald MacLeish, 1917–1982,* 37 *Western Humanities Review,* September 1988, 268–69, wrote to much the same effect: "Each career fed into the other, but also blocked the total commitment that leads to fulfillment. As lawyer he was too idealistic and emotional; as poet, he was too judicial and intellectually aware."

90 *Letters of Archibald MacLeish, supra* note 1, at 334 (letter dated 19 October 1945): "What you and . . . I talked about . . . was the Republic and the obligation to serve it. Never after that hour, except from you, did I ever hear from anyone talk of the obligation to serve the Republic. I hear only the opposite—talk colored by the universally accepted assumption that it was not for that reason but for other reasons that men were in Government in Washington. . . . I am talking about the assumption of better men that it was in some way naïve or unsophisticated or uninformed to attribute to the wish to serve the Republic what could conceivably be attributed to other impulses. You and you alone— and this is not the least of my reasons for loving you—have dared to believe that men do enter Government . . . because they believe in the Republic and wish to serve it."

91 *Uphill with Archie, supra* note 1, at 124.

92 Donaldson, *supra* note 1, at 216–19, quoting Hemingway as saying that Archie had nothing left to work for "except the Nobel Prize, the French Academy and Westminster abbey—MacLeish a success at last—From the training table to a seat with the immortals."

93 David Barber, *In Search of an "Image of Mankind": The Public Poetry and Prose of Archibald MacLeish,* 29 *American Studies* 55 n. 54 (1988). See also Donaldson, *supra* note 1, at 195, 277; "Archibald MacLeish Is Dead: Poet and Playwright Was 89," *New York Times,* 21 April 1982, § A, p. 1 (describing *Fortune* as "then a sort of gadfly to the business world").

94 See, for example, his "Public Speech," "Frescoes for Mr. Rockefeller's City," and "America Was Promises," all written during this period.

95 E.g., "The Irresponsibles" (1940), 9 ("They have seen the crisis of their time. . . . And yet they continue to pretend that they do not know"), 21 ("The men of intellectual duty . . . have divided themselves into two castes, two cults—the scholars and the writers. Neither accepts responsibility for the common culture or its defense"). MacLeish first delivered "The Irresponsibles" as an address to the American Philosophical Society on 19 April 1940. He later published it in the *Nation* (18 May 1940, 618) and as a short book in 1940, and still later defended it in an address at Smith College (1953), pointing out that slavery and despotism produced no great art; that liberty is the precondition of artistic creation; and that artists have an obligation to defend it. "On

'The Irresponsibles' " (Library of Congress, Manuscript Division, MacLeish File).

96 MacLeish's disputes with his critics also had a literary criticism dimension, having to do with contending theories of both poetry and criticism, which we do not explore here. See John Timberman Newcomb, "Archibald MacLeish and the Poetics of Public Speech: A Critique of High Modernism," 29 *Journal of the Midwest Modern Language Association* 9 (1990); Frank A. Ninkovich, "The New Criticism and Cold War America," 20 *Southern Quarterly* 1 (1981).

97 Donaldson, *supra* note 1, at 334–38; *Uphill with Archie, supra* note 1, at 124–25 (noting that MacLeish, in "The Irresponsibles," seemingly forgot that he himself had earlier railed against the inanity of war).

98 "The Irresponsibles," *supra* note 95, at 25–33.

99 "Public Speech and Private Speech in Poetry," *A Time to Speak: The Selected Prose of Archibald MacLeish* (1941), 63–65. See also "Poetry and the Public World," *supra* note 61, at 92–94. On MacLeish's switch of position, see Donaldson, *supra* note 1, at 288, 460 (writing that for MacLeish, the purpose of poetry was expressing resonant truths about the world).

100 "The Irresponsibles," *supra* note 95, at 21–25. On Kronman's critique see part II.

101 Archibald MacLeish, Foreword, *Felix Frankfurter, Law and Politics: Occasional Papers of Felix Frankfurter, 1913–1938* (Archibald MacLeish & E. F. Prichard eds., 1939), xiii.

102 See "Post-War Writers and Pre-War Readers," *New Republic,* 10 June 1940, 789–90 (naming Hemingway a "pacifist" and John Dos Passos a man contemptuous of conviction).

103 Donaldson, *supra* note 1, at 274.

104 *Panic* played in 1935, *Fall of the City* in 1937, *Air Raid* in 1938.

105 Malcolm Cowley, "Men and Ghosts," 82 *New Republic,* 27 March 1935, 90–91. Cowley commended him, however, for transcending the theme of personal isolation and reaching a new audience in *The Fall of the City.* Indeed, the play was thought to have been heard by one million listeners on the radio.

106 In the 1920s MacLeish was greatly preoccupied with self, time, immortality, meaning, and the nature of reality. For example, an entry from his notebook (probably spring 1925) observes: "We are taught to live inwardly in continued judgment upon ourselves, self conscious. We are taught to examine ourselves to see that we conform to a law or to the expectations of others. . . . The important thing is self-respect. . . . The question is not what am I life. But, What, Life, are you?" (Library of Congress, Manuscript Division, MacLeish File).

107 Mason Wade, "The Anabasis of A. MacLeish," 243 *North American Review* 330 (June 1937); Swanberg, *supra* note 75, at 137–41; Donaldson, *supra* note 1, at 278.

108   Donaldson, *supra* note 1, at 276–80.

109   *Id.* at 290–91, 358–65; *Letters of Archibald MacLeish, supra* note 1, at xiv–xv. Although his service in the latter job was controversial, he won widespread recognition as a successful director of the library, modernizing fiscal and administrative procedures, increasing holdings, and winning salary increases for the staff.

110   *Letters of Archibald MacLeish, supra* note 1, at 307–9, 318–21 (letters to Henry Luce dated 13 February 1942, to James Allen dated 12 October 1943). See also letter to Claude Barnett (5 March 1942) (Library of Congress, Manuscript Division, MacLeish File) (describing plans for a conference to line up Negro support for the war effort). In later life, MacLeish spoke ruefully about his role as a propagandist. See *Archibald MacLeish: Reflections, supra* note 1, at 155. See also Archibald MacLeish, "Propaganda: Good and Bad" (1947) (roundtable) (Library of Congress, Manuscript Division, MacLeish File) ("[Y]ou can't talk about the whole truth . . . unless you define your terms").

111   *Letters of Archibald MacLeish, supra* note 1, at 319–20 (letter to James Allen dated 12 October 1943); Donaldson, *supra* note 1, at 351–54 (MacLeish enthusiastically accepted role of apologist for U.S. war effort). In one way of looking at things, Pound and MacLeish were opposite numbers—MacLeish a propagandist for the United States, Pound a propagandist for the fascist Italian government.

112   *Uphill with Archie, supra* note 1, at 153 (paraphrasing MacLeish's address at the inauguration of Freedom House, 19 March 1942; reprinted in *A Time to Act*).

113   *Id.* at 154.

114   C. David Heymann, "The Pound Files," *New York Times*, 21 April 1974, § 7, p. 47. MacLeish and others cooperated with FBI inquiries after Pound was indicted. Paul L. Montgomery, "Scholar Gets F.B.I. File on Ezra Pound," *New York Times*, 10 March 1974, 40.

115   *Letters of Archibald MacLeish, supra* note 1, at 317–18 (letter dated 10 September 1943) (suggesting to Harvey Bundy, assistant secretary of war, that Pound be treated in the same manner as the Civil War traitor Clement C. Vallandingham, who after trial by a military commission was discharged into exile); see Ex parte Vallandingham, 68 U.S. (1 Wall.) 243 (1863).

116   Donaldson, *supra* note 1, at 368.

117   *Letters of Archibald MacLeish, supra* note 1, at 329 (letter dated 18 May 1945). MacLeish told Eliot that Pound had been indicted in absentia for treason and would be returned to the United States for trial. To another query about Pound, MacLeish replied that the poet was still detained in Italy, where his behavior suggested that a psychiatric examination was in order. He further stated that Pound had written to the attorney general admitting the charges

but insisting that the broadcasts had been protected speech. *Id.* at 330 (letter dated 13 August 1945). See also Henry Meacham, *The Caged Panther: Ezra Pound at Saint Elizabeths* (1967), 22 (reporting that Pound insisted that he broadcast not to help the fascists but to educate the American people and bring them the truth).

118 Donaldson, *supra* note 1, at 392.

119 C. Norman, *The Case of Ezra Pound* (1968), 103; E. Torrey, *The Roots of Treason: Ezra Pound and the Secrets of St. Elizabeths* (1984), 186–91.

120 *Letters of Archibald MacLeish*, *supra* note 1, at 335–36 (letter dated 6 December 1945). Earlier, Cornell had expressly authorized MacLeish to visit Pound (letter dated 24 November 1945) (Library of Congress, Manuscript Division, MacLeish File).

121 *Letters of Archibald MacLeish*, *supra* note 1, at 336–37. See also Letter from Ezra Pound to Shakespear and Parkyn (5 October 1945) (Library of Congress, Manuscript Division, MacLeish File). At the same time that MacLeish was distancing himself from Pound, Pound was determined to make MacLeish his lawyer. In the letter to Eliot, MacLeish refers to a copy of a letter that Eliot had enclosed from Pound to his London solicitor insisting: "Emphatically I want to see Mr. McLeish [*sic*]. . . . But the simplest plan would be for him to write to me as my lawyer (if I am correct in supposing that he is a lawyer) at any rate he has known my work for 20 years and has some concept of what I have been driving at."

122 He told Julien Cornell that his day and a half in Washington turned out to be too busy. *Letters of Archibald MacLeish*, *supra* note 1, at 335–36 (letter dated 6 December 1945). However, later he was to regret it: "I should have [visited Pound] years ago, but just plain lacked the stomach. I hate asylums and I'd only met Pound once in my life in any case and so I let my conscience sleep." Humphrey Carpenter, *A Serious Character: The Life of Ezra Pound* (1988), 818.

123 Donaldson, *supra* note 1, at 396; *Uphill with Archie*, *supra* note 1, at 164 (reporting that MacLeish was depressed during this period).

124 Donaldson, *supra* note 1, at 398.

125 *Id.* at 399–400.

126 See C. David Heymann, *Ezra Pound: The Last Rower: A Political Profile* (1976), 218–21; Torrey, *supra* note 119, at 234–46. See also Ninkovich, *supra* note 96, at 3–20 (on the controversy in general and MacLeish's role in it).

127 Donaldson, *supra* note 1, at 404–15. MacLeish had a rough start as a teacher. Some of his students, including Donald Hall and Robert Bly, perhaps thinking that MacLeish was too patrician and owed his job to his political connections, challenged him in the classroom. But in typical fashion, after some soul-searching he changed his teaching method, meeting his seminar students indi-

vidually. The system seems to have worked; later, Bly and Hall acknowledged their debt to MacLeish. In his lecture class, MacLeish devised a system requiring each student to jot down on a note card a few reflections on the next day's readings, and turn in the card on the day before class. MacLeish would then produce the pack of cards at the beginning of the class, pick out one, and read aloud what it contained. He would then go on to the next, all in an order he had previously selected to develop the ideas he needed to address. The class would then discuss the ideas of the student commentators, taking the focus off MacLeish and giving the students a larger role in the instruction. Donaldson, *supra* note 1, at 400–14, 416. See *Uphill with Archie, supra* note 4, at 17 (MacLeish's classes became standing room only).

128 *Letters of Archibald MacLeish, supra* note 1, at 344–46 (letter to Harrison Smith, publisher of the *Saturday Review of Literature,* dated 27 May 1949).

129 (1950).

130 *Id.* at 47.

131 Ninkovich, *supra* note 96, at 19–20 (ascribing this position to MacLeish). See also Donaldson, *supra* note 1, at 443 (arguing that MacLeish miscited Aristotle).

132 See Donaldson, *supra* note 1, at 399–400 (on MacLeish's attitude toward witch hunts in general); *Uphill with Archie, supra* note 1, at 154 (attributing to MacLeish the view that U.S. totalitarianism would need to be unusually brutal to quell a citizenry accustomed to freedom).

133 Jeffrey Meyers, "Shrinking Pound," *Spectator,* 28 April 1984.

134 Donaldson, *supra* note 1, at 432. "On October 9 [1952] MacLeish, Arthur M. Schlesinger, Sr., and Mark DeWolfe Howe announced a nationwide fundraising effort aimed at unseating McCarthy." A few weeks later, McCarthy retaliated by accusing Adlai Stevenson, the Democratic presidential nominee, of harboring "advisors whose loyalty was in question," including MacLeish, who was Stevenson's speechwriter. He charged MacLeish with having "been affiliated with as vast a number of communist fronts, according to the Un-American Activities Committee, as any other individual whom I have ever named."

135 Archibald MacLeish, "A Retiring View of Harvard," *Harvard Alumni Bulletin,* 12 January 1963, 309–11. See also Donaldson, *supra* note 1, at 432–33.

136 Howard Zinn, *The Twentieth Century: A People's History* (1984), 128–31.

137 On 1 January 1953 MacLeish began the new year with a letter to the Harvard provost, Paul Buck. Because MacLeish would be on leave and out of the country in the fall of that year, he wanted Buck to have a record of his political and literary actions during the previous twenty-five years. Stressing his Americanism and loyalty, he submitted a detailed list. *Letters of Archibald MacLeish,*

supra note 1, at 363–67. Because McCarthy had accused him, just a short time earlier, of belonging to communist front organizations, MacLeish may have feared that this association with Pound might come to light and cause trouble of a different sort. Note the irony: "He was called a fascist by communists and a communist by Senator Joseph McCarthy," Winnick, Introduction, *Letters of Archibald MacLeish, supra* note 1, at xi. MacLeish's fears may have been reasonable. See Irving Wallace, David Wallechinsky, and Amy Wallace, "Writers Who Were Watched by the FBI," *San Francisco Chronicle*, 17 January 1990, § B, p. 3 (FBI maintained a file on MacLeish, whom J. Edgar Hoover considered a "liberal of the New Deal type"). And MacLeish suffered vicious red-baiting during his confirmation hearings for director of the Library of Congress, Donaldson, *supra* note 1, at 295–97.

MacLeish may have flirted briefly with communism in the 1930s, although he later denounced it and became a staunch patriot. See, e.g., "In Our Time: The Industrial Civilization of New York Seen in the Cross Section of a Diego Rivera Fresco," *Fortune*, February 1932, 41 (criticizing communism for forcing artists to choose between ideology and art). (But note that although he did not recognize it, capitalism imposed a similar choice on him: art or law.) See also Wade, "The Anabasis of A. MacLeish," *supra* note 107, at 330 (describing MacLeish as uninterested in communism and mass movements in general); Donaldson, *supra* note 1, at 288 (same).

138 Pound's daughter believed that the timing of the renewed relationship was not coincidental. See De Rachewiltz, *Indiscretions, supra* note 73, at 294 (positing that the fear of McCarthyism silenced Pound's friends and kept them from coming to his rescue).

139 *Letters of Archibald MacLeish, supra* note 1, at 377–78 (letters dated August 1955, 18 August 1955, September 1955).

140 *Id.* at 378 (letter dated 18 August 1955).

141 Archibald MacLeish, "In Praise of Dissent," *New York Times*, 16 December 1956, § 7, p. 5.

142 Pound was not the perfect hero-in-distress; he could be fractious. See *Letters of Archibald MacLeish, supra* note 1, at 384–85 (letter to Ezra Pound dated 5 July 1956) (MacLeish tells Pound he would like to get him out on a medical basis, but Pound insists on telling "the truth" to the public); Carpenter, *supra* note 122, at 820 (1988) (same). See also Heymann, *supra* note 126, at 236, quoting Pound's letters to MacLeish. 30 July 1956: "What the Hell do you read? Where has yr/paideuma got to re 'Brain Washing'? Have you read Benton and Blackstone? How many years of anything are you willing to read at MY recommendation . . . ? I should have at least a little factual indication that your mind is opening to the possibilities of even yr/adored dunghill F.D.R. having erred a

few points in his judgment both of the world situation and in his choice of associates." 6 August 1956: "Wars are made to make DEBT and yr/old fuehrer's war was BLOODY successful. . . . Have you read testimony of army, navy and marines?? Can't make out what, if anything, you DO read." And finally, 18 December 1956: "Can I get yu to see that in 30 years you have NEVER mentioned to me ANY specific point on which you respect anyone's opinion. And when I call a louse a louse / a seller or giver of currency plates to the enemy / a cheater of the people re / price of gold, you never reply with anything specific. . . . In yr / great fog, come on, and name some SINGLE definition, some single buzzard among the mutts whom you have drifted among who will come clean on a PARTICULAR statement, or stand up against a particular accusation of error."

143 *Letters of Archibald MacLeish, supra* note 1, at 392–94, 395, 397–99, 401 (letters dated 15 December 1956, 8 January 1957, 14 January 1957, 3 June 1957, 19 June 1957, 21 July 1957). See Meacham, *supra* note 117, at 93 (when Hemingway accepted the Nobel Prize for literature he pleaded for Pound's release).

144 *Letters of Archibald MacLeish, supra* note 1, at 395 (letter to Hemingway dated 3 June 1957).

145 *Id.* at 395–96, 399–400 (letter to Hemingway dated 3 June 1957; letters to Frost dated 28 June 1957, 9 July 1957). According to some accounts, Frost received credit for achieving Pound's release, but a fair reading of the record shows that MacLeish's efforts were more influential. See Lawrance Thompson and R. H. Winnick, *Robert Frost: The Later Years, 1938–63* (1976), 247–58.

146 Torrey, *supra* note 119, at 254–55, 326 n. 135.

147 Heymann, *supra* note 126, at 244; Meacham, *supra* note 117, at 114.

148 *Letters of Archibald MacLeish, supra* note 1, at 407 (letter to Ezra Pound dated 30 March 1958); Meacham, *supra* note 117, at 113, 123 (Herter invoked international sentiment to persuade the U.S. State Department to intercede).

149 Torrey, *supra* note 119, at 255, 326 n. 135; Heymann, *supra* note 126, at 244–45.

150 Donald Hall, *Remembering Poets: Reminiscences and Opinions: Dylan Thomas, Robert Frost, T. S. Eliot, Ezra Pound* (1978), 59.

151 Meacham, *supra* note 117, at 126 (Indictment dropped ["nol pros"] on the ground that the government could never prove Pound's sanity during the war years; Pound's case was argued by Thurman Arnold. Arnold was a former student of Pound's from his short-lived teaching stint at Wabash College.). See also Heymann, *supra* note 126, at 254–55 (Justice Department agreed not to oppose nol pros motion).

152 See Carpenter, *supra* note 122, at 896: "Such few letters as he now wrote were succinct, courteous, and neat, in fountain pen or ballpoint. On 10 April 1967

he sent this note to Laughlin about the publication of a limited edition of one of his early poems . . . : 'Dear Jas, All right, go ahead. It reeks with conceit. It needs punctuation. I want to correct the proofs. I can still sign my own name. Yours E.P. Ezra Pound Ezra Pound (nine times). Conceit remains.' "

153 Torrey, *supra* note 119, at 261–83 (chapter 9, "After the Fall: Venice, 1958– 1972") (Pound, despondent, believed himself a failure and considered anti-Semitism to have been his greatest mistake). He also repented his mistreatment of MacLeish, writing to him: "Forgive me for about 80% of the violent things I have said about some of your friends, . . . it is probably too late to retract 'em. . . . Violent language is an error. I did not get full of Agassiz. That might have saved me. Whether my errors can be useful to others, God knows." And: "I merely tried to get a few points across and get concrete answers to questions that NEED answers,. . . . I am broken by not being able to get any serious answers. . . . That ain't yr/fault." Twelve years later, only four months before Pound's death, MacLeish responded, through a letter to Meacham: "Tell Ezra when next you write that I love him. He won't like it, but he has no choice." Heymann, *supra* note 126, at 270.

Even before this time, Pound felt misgivings over his harsh treatment of MacLeish. In 1956, while discussing with MacLeish how best to get himself out, Pound wrote to MacLeish: "It wd/be a pity were we to die without explaining ourselves to each other." Letter from Ezra Pound to Archibald MacLeish (27 June 1956) (Library of Congress, Manuscript Division, MacLeish File). A decade later, expressing regret for a rude remark attributed to him, he wrote: "This was published without my knowledge and would never have had my consent. I can't remember what it was all about and no longer feel that kind of thing of importance. What is of importance is an old and tried friendship. I should be sorry to have this brought to your attention by anybody else. I think you know my epistolary habits too well to take it seriously." Carpenter, *supra* note 122, at 896 (letter dated 2 March 1967).

154 E.g., Letter from Archibald MacLeish to Ezra Pound (26 October 1957) (Library of Congress, Manuscript Division, MacLeish File) ("I am doing what I am doing partly because I revere you and partly because I love this Republic and can't be quiet when it violates its own convictions").

155 MacLeish also wrote speeches for Roosevelt and Adlai Stevenson. See Helen E. Ellis and Bernard A. Drabeck, *Archibald MacLeish: A Selectively Annotated Bibliography* (1995), xv; Donaldson, *supra* note 1, at 341–43, 366 (Roosevelt), 430–31 (Stevenson). He also wrote the Preamble to the United Nations Charter. Donaldson, *supra* note 1, at 388.

156 By "legal talents" we mean advocacy on behalf of a single client, rather than the country as a whole. MacLeish's advocacy on behalf of Pound took the form

of writing letters, making calls, and conducting meetings with key members of government—all classic tasks of a well-placed lawyer. At times, he expressly coordinated his work with Pound's attorneys of record, Julien Cornell and Thurman Arnold. See letter from Archibald MacLeish to Ezra Pound (7 September 1955) (Beinecke Library Collection) (custody of Yale University Collection) ("As for the law—I haven't practiced it for more than thirty years but I have no doubts on that proposition. Anyone who told you different was lost in a private fog").

157 E.g., Letter from Archibald MacLeish to Ezra Pound (1 September 1956) (Beinecke Library Collection) (custody of Yale University Collection) ("I refer not only to y[ou]r blasts at me on Rome radio . . . but to the letter you composed when I sent you the [lines] of a poem of mine called You Andrew Marvell for *Exile*. Boy! My skin don't blister no mo.' No sir, boss man, she is fried"); *id*. (14 October 1956) ("You are right about you and me and Persia—though I don't think the poem was merely decorative. But you are right. I have been reading your tr[anslation] of the Odes and how right you are").

158 MacLeish was on a first-name basis with Felix Frankfurter, Dean Acheson, Franklin Roosevelt, Henry Luce, Milton Eisenhower, and many others. Professor Felix Frankfurter of Harvard Law School channeled the best and brightest Harvard Law graduates and Supreme Court clerks into government service. Arthur M. Schlesinger Jr., *The Politics of Upheaval* (1960), 225. His teaching undoubtedly influenced MacLeish, a quintessential New Deal man. Like his mentors, he valued the free market system for the opportunities it provided citizens to shape their lives and plan their destinies. Because concentration of specialized and technical expertise removed power from participants in a democracy, it was essential, in Frankfurter's view, that government service attract those who could bring to it the benefits of liberal education. *Id*. at 223. Much of the writing of the time referred to government as "the Republic" and had a highly Jeffersonian flavor. It also reflected a detestation of communism and socialism. *Id*.

MacLeish was among the elect early in life. Two-thirds of his graduating class at Hotchkiss went to Yale. Donaldson, *supra* note 1, at 31.

159 Carpenter, *supra* note 122, at 825–26. See also MacLeish, *Riders on the Earth*, *supra* note 1, at 120 (noting that the United States at this time was criticizing the Soviets for their abuse of psychiatry); De Rachewiltz, *supra* note 138, at 299 (same). At the same time, the insanity defense was being broadened, see Durham v. United States, 214 F.2d 862 (D.C. Cir. 1954), *overruled*, 471 F.2d 969, 981 (D.C. Cir. 1972). If Pound had been tried under the liberal Durham standard, he might well have been acquitted as insane. The Department of Justice might have encountered additional difficulties in convicting Pound.

The crime of treason—"adhering" to the nation's enemies and giving them aid and comfort—required testimony by two witnesses; but the Italian radio technicians who were present during Pound's broadcasts spoke no English. See Torrey, *supra* note 119, at 179–80 (citing government memorandum acknowledging this and other obstacles in the case against Pound). Yet the nation's mood required retribution, *id.* at 180. Pound's friends, realizing the high chance of a conviction and possible death penalty, suggested a medical-insanity plea and also one of incompetence to stand trial. Heymann, *supra* note 126, at 190–91. Pound was manifestly clear-headed and sane, as evidenced by his lucid letter to Attorney General Francis Biddle about the reasons for his Italian actions. *Id.* at 136–38. Yet the government agreed to his commitment, perhaps as a compromise, believing its position weak. Torrey, *supra* note 119, at 218.

160 See S. Kutler, *The American Inquisition: Justice and Injustice in the Cold War* (1982), 74–80; Torrey, *supra* note 119, at 248–51.

161 Torrey, *supra* note 119, at 238–42 (describing mistresses or love servants devoted to bringing out what Pound describes as "a fine rapacious beastie"). Others made sure he had the materials that he needed to write. See Carpenter, *supra* note 122, at 818 (MacLeish arranged for the Library of Congress to send books to the inmate).

162 See text and notes immediately *supra* (noting that fear of McCarthyism made the cautious MacLeish even more reluctant to act than usual). See also his letter to Pound, in *Letters of Archibald MacLeish*, *supra* note 1, at 379 (letter dated 3 March 1956) ("If you have read anything you've been reading McCarthy"); Letter from Archibald MacLeish to Ezra Pound (23 June 1956) (Beinecke Library Collection) (custody of Yale University Collection) ("I am NOT determined to chuck the US Constitution down the drain: on the contrary, it's the one roof I want to live under and I have spent a lot of time and effort trying to hold it up against the McCarthys and the Commies and the rest of that kidney"); *id.* (1 September 1956) ("The nastiest thing in the history of the Republic was the sick-minded effort to find Communists under every bed in Washington in order to discourage humans from thinking and acting like men"); Letter from Ezra Pound to Archibald MacLeish (19 February 1957) (Library of Congress, Manuscript Division, MacLeish File) ("Who is McCarthy?").

163 See "An American Storyteller," *Time*, 12 December 1954, 72.

164 347 U.S. 483 (1954).

165 See Carpenter, *supra* note 122, at 827–29; Torrey, *supra* note 119, at 255; Editorial, "An Artist Confined: Artists at Liberty," *Life*, 6 February 1956, 30 (advocating Pound's release in light of changed social conditions); "An American Storyteller," *supra* note 163, at 72 (interview with Hemingway).

166 See Mary Dudziak, *Cold War Civil Rights* (2002); Mary Dudziak, *Desegregation*

as a Cold War Imperative, 41 *Stanford Law Review* 61 (1988) (both citing State Department correspondence and similar memoranda showing that the U.S. government wanted the Justice Department to work for a major victory for blacks in order to advance its cold war objectives and burnish America's image overseas). MacLeish had served as assistant secretary of state in the immediate postwar years and must have been aware of the connection between domestic troubles and America's ability to exercise leadership in the uncommitted Third World. The decision in *Brown* promoted both black justice and America's foreign policy interests. Pound's release only promoted the latter and so was a calculated gamble. He might have remained in the United States and made anti-black and anti-Semitic statements, compounding problems for the diplomatic sector. Fortunately, he returned almost immediately to Italy, whose shores he greeted with an unrepentant fascist salute. Heymann, *supra* note 126, at 257 (citing Pound's words: "All America is an insane asylum").

167   As early as 1922, MacLeish exhibited a Realist awareness. In the poem "The Lord Chancellor Prepares His Opinion," the young lawyer describes a magistrate's ruling against a beautiful woman who had brought suit to stop the display of a painting of herself after she refused payment to the artist. The magistrate cites legal authority, although the case could have gone either way. But an interior monologue reveals that the judge ruled as he did because of passion: he has seen the painting, was swept away by it, and wants to look at it again.

168   Legal realism, in short, might have enabled him to connect the technical practice of law with the richness of the world as he experienced it. A few lawyer-poets seem to have escaped or shrugged off this form of law-school brainwashing. Why? Perhaps it was more intense at Harvard than elsewhere. Or perhaps some were able to compartmentalize better than MacLeish was, keeping their business ("day job") lives separate from their poetry. See chapter 7, *infra*, at note 7 and accompanying text (discussing Wallace Stevens).

3 Formalism

1   See chapter 2, *supra* (describing MacLeish's life in relation to legal developments at Harvard and elsewhere).

2   See, e.g., Richard Pildes, "Forms of Formalism," 66 *University of Chicago Law Review* 607 (1999) (describing formalism as anticonsequential morality in legal reasoning; as a purposive rule-following; and as a regulatory tool for producing optimally efficient mixes of law and norms in contract law, for example). Pildes's essay introduces a small group of articles setting out the virtues and defects of various types of formalism. See Symposium, "Roots of Formalism,"

66 *University of Chicago Law Review*, supra, including articles by Cass Sunstein, William Eskridge, Larry Alexander, Daniel Farber, and others.

3 For a classic defense, see Ernest J. Weinrib, "Legal Formalism: On the Immanent Rationality of Law," 97 *Yale Law Journal* 949 (1988). See also Robert S. Summers, *How Law Is Formal and Why It Matters*, 82 *Cornell Law Review* 1165 (1977); Lyrissa Lidsky, "Defensor Fidel: The Travails of a Post-Realist Formalist," 47 *Florida Law Review* 815 (1995). On a somewhat related phenomenon, see Lisa Ruddock, "The Near Enemy of the Humanities Is Professionalism," *Chronicle of Higher Education*, 23 November 2001, § B, p. 7 (observing that rigid rules and norms in various professions inhibit innovation, stifle creativity, and are ultimately anti-humanistic).

4 Weinrib, *supra* note 3. See also Laura Kalman, *Legal Realism at Yale, 1927–1960* (1986).

5 On these tiers of constitutional scrutiny, see, e.g., Laurence Tribe, *American Constitutional Law* (2d ed. 1988) (setting out various models of constitutional analysis according to the area in question and the type of case). See also Richard A. Posner, "Legal Formalism, Legal Realism, and the Interpretation of Statutes and the Constitution," 37 *Case Western Reserve Law Review* 179 (1987) (arguing that formalism, like its opposite, realism, has no place in the interpretation of statutes and constitutional provisions, but that elsewhere judges are free to select common law premises in accord with social policy and pragmatism; formalism would come into play when judges reason deductively from these premises to conclusions in particular cases).

6 See Lidsky, *supra* note 3; Posner, *supra* note 5 (arguing that no extrinsic concerns—only interpretive tools—can be brought to bear in interpreting statutes).

7 But it does. Social scientists who studied Supreme Court opinions found that one could predict the result more accurately by knowing the justices' biases and political leanings than by knowing the precedents that bore on the cases. See, e.g., Jeffrey A. Segal, *The Supreme Court and the Attitudinal Model* (1993).

8 See Weinrib, *supra* note 3.

9 See Chris Goodrich, *Anarchy and Elegance: Confessions of a Journalist at Yale Law School* (1991) (commenting on the disjunction between law's elegant theories and the buzzing, confusing world of facts, disputes, and clients).

10 Josef Redlich, *The Common Law and the Case Method in American University Law Schools* (1914). See also Mark Warren Bailey, "Early Legal Education in the United States: Natural Law Theory and Law as a Moral Science," 48 *Journal of Legal Education* 311, 312 (1998).

11 See John Henry Schlegel, "Between the Harvard Founders and the American Legal Realists: The Professionalization of the American Law Professor," 35 *Journal of Legal Education* 311 (1985); Elizabeth Mensch, "The History of

Mainstream Legal Thought," *The Politics of Law* (David Kairys ed., 2d ed. 1990); Pierre Schlag, "Normative and Nowhere to Go," 43 *Stanford Law Review* 167, 180 (1990) (all commenting on the origins, political underpinnings, and decline of mechanical jurisprudence and—in Schlag's case—its recent resurgence).

12   C. C. Langdell, "Teaching Law as a Science," 21 *American Law Review* 123, 123 (1887).

13   See Andrew Abbott, *The System of Professions* (1988), 55–56; Maxwell H. Bloomfield, "Law: The Development of a Profession," *The Professions in American History* (Nathan O. Hatch ed., 1988), 33; Richard Abel, *American Lawyers* (1989). On Langdell's own drive for professionalization, see Bruce A. Kimball, "Young Christopher Langdell, 1826–54: The Formation of an Educational Reformer," 52 *Journal of Legal Education* 189, 237 (2002).

14   See Kalman, *supra* note 4; Richard Delgado and Jean Stefancic, *Critical Race Theory: An Introduction* (2002) (tracing origins of contemporary legal movements in legal realism). See also Archibald MacLeish, Foreword, *Felix Frankfurter: Law and Politics: Occasional Papers of Felix Frankfurter, 1913–1938* (Archibald MacLeish & E. F. Prichard eds., 1939), x ("In so far as these [legal] questions are necessarily questions of fact . . . it is essential that the stream of the Zeitgeist be allowed to flood the sympathies and the intelligence of our judges. This is necessary, not only for the well-being of the state and the social order, but for the unimpaired continuance of our judicial system.") (quoting Felix Frankfurter), xviii (citing Holmes to the same effect), xix (same, citing Brandeis).

15   See Duncan Kennedy, "The Structure of Blackstone's Commentaries," 28 *Buffalo Law Review* 209 (1979).

16   Delgado and Stefancic, *supra* note 14. See also Gary Minda, *Postmodern Legal Movements: Law and Jurisprudence at Century's End* (1995).

17   For a vivid novelistic portrayal, see, e.g., Scott Turow, *One L* (1977). On the method's continuing popularity, see, e.g., David D. Garner, "The Continuing Vitality of the Case Method in the Twenty-First Century," 2000 *BYU Education and Law Journal* 307; Deborah L. Rhode, "Kicking the Socratic Method and Other Reforms for Law Schools," *Chronicle of Higher Education*, 26 January 2001, § B, p. 15.

18   E.g., Brown v. Board of Education, 347 U.S. 483 (1954).

19   See R.A.V. v. City of St. Paul, 505 U.S. 377 (1992) (deciding a cross-burning case almost exclusively by reference to First Amendment categories and with little consideration of racial history, lynching, the Ku Klux Klan, the rise of skinheads, or the effects of terrorism on black families like the victims).

20   Weinrib, *supra* note 3, at 949.

21   Lidsky, *supra* note 3, at 822.

22 E.g., *id.* at 822.

23 *Id.* at 827 (describing Robert Summers).

24 See chapters 4 and 5, *infra* (on lawyers' lives and recent changes in law practice).

25 Maoism, for example. In most disciplines, formalism is associated with an élitist conception of scholarship, an emphasis on tradition, imperialistic, pro-Western politics, and neoliberal or conservative leanings. See, e.g., Norman Cantor, *Inventing the Middle Ages* (1991), 161–204.

26 See R.A.V. v. City of St. Paul, 505 U.S. 377 (1992).

27 See Robert M. Cover, "Violence and the Word," 95 *Yale Law Journal* 1601 (1986); Robert M. Cover, "Nomos and Narrative," 97 *Harvard Law Review* 4 (1983) (both describing the coercive, sometimes violent character of judicial proceedings).

28 Plessy v. Ferguson, 163 U.S. 537 (1896).

29 Lochner v. New York, 198 U.S. 45 (1905).

30 See Maria Fleming, "The Strike for Three Loaves," *A Place at the Table: Struggles for Equality in America* (Southern Poverty Law Center 2000), 57.

31 300 U.S. 379 (1937). See also Nebbia v. New York, 291 U.S. 502 (1934). We thank Omar Swartz for calling this period to our attention.

32 See *Plessy*, 163 U.S. 537 (1896) (discussed *supra*).

33 Brown v. Board of Education, 347 U.S. 483 (1954).

34 See Gerald Rosenberg, *The Hollow Hope: Can Courts Bring About Social Change?* (1991).

35 Rosenberg, *supra* note 34.

36 73 *Harvard Law Review* 1 (1959).

37 "The Path of the Law," 10 *Harvard Law Review* 457, 469 (1897).

38 See, e.g., James Boyd White, *The Legal Imagination: Studies in the Nature of Legal Thought and Expression* (1973), and *Heracles' Bow: Essays on the Rhetoric and Poetics of the Law* (1985).

39 See "Legal Education and Professional Development: An Educational Continuum," 1992 *A.B.A. Section on Legal Education and Admissions to the Bar* (containing findings of the A.B.A. Task Force on Law Schools and the Profession: Narrowing the Gap, chaired by Robert MacCrate). See also Robert MacCrate, "Paradigm Lost—or Revised and Regained?," 38 *Journal of Legal Education* 295 (1988).

40 91 *Michigan Law Review* 34 (1992).

41 "My point is simply that the function of the first-year classes, rightly understood, is to create in students the capacity to understand and use the full range of legal doctrine." *Id.* at 58. See Pierre Schlag, "Ten Thousand Cases, Maybe More: An Essay on Centrism in Legal Education," 2 *Agora* 2 (2002) ("For the most part, law school teaching is organized around the review, dissection and

assimilation of judicial opinions. . . . approximately 10,000 cases over a three-year period").

42 See McClesky v. Kemp, 481 U.S. 279 (1987), upholding Georgia's administration of capital sentencing, in the face of social scientists' findings that it grossly discriminated against African Americans, especially those whose victims were white. David C. Baldus, George Woodworth, and Charles A. Pulaski Jr., *Equal Justice and the Death Penalty: A Legal and Empirical Analysis* (1991), 370–80. For a death penalty case that exemplifies formalism taken to a perverse extreme see Singleton v. Norris, 319 F.3d 1018, 2003 US. App. LEXIS 2198 (8th Cir. 2003), cert. denied, 124 S. Ct. 74, in which the court upheld the forced medication of a mentally incompetent death row prisoner so that he could be made sane enough to be executed. The court explained, apparently without irony, that from the prisoner's perspective "[e]ligibility for execution is the only unwanted consequence of the medication."

43 See Ruth Colker and James J. Brudney, "Dissing Congress," 100 *Michigan Law Review* 80 (2001); Ruth Colker and Kevin M. Scott, "Dissing States," 88 *Virginia Law Review* 1301 (2002).

44 E.g., United States v. Morrison, 529 U.S. 598 (2000). By federalism we mean states' rights; by original intent, deference to the constitutional framers; and by textualism, literal adherence to the language rather than the spirit of a statute.

45 490 U.S. 642 (1989).

46 488 U.S. 469 (1989).

47 McClesky v. Kemp, 481 U.S. 279 (1987). The "Baldus Study," which lawyers for the challenger introduced, controlled for 240 variables.

4 Lawyers and Their Discontents

1 Susan Daicoff, "Asking Leopards to Change Their Spots: Should Lawyers Change? A Critique of Solutions to Problems with Professionalism by Reference to Empirically-Derived Attorney Personality Attributes," 11 *Georgetown Journal of Legal Ethics* 547 (1998); "Lawyer, Know Thyself: A Review of Empirical Research on Attorney Attributes Bearing on Professionalism," 46 *American University Law Review* 1337 (1997) (both articles discussing personality traits and characteristics of lawyers and law students).

2 See Walter Bennett, *The Lawyer's Myth, Reviving Ideals in the Legal Profession* (2001) (calling attention to role of myths in determining professional identity and aspiration).

3 Deborah Rhode, *In the Interests of Justice: Reforming the Legal Profession* (2001) (putting forward wide-ranging critique of current state of legal profession).

4 Mary Ann Glendon, *A Nation Under Lawyers: How the Crisis in Legal Education is Transforming American Society* (1994), 152–73, 190.

5 *Id.* at 40–59.

6 Anthony Kronman, *The Lost Lawyer: Failing Ideals of the Legal Profession* (1993) (showing how lawyers have lost the high ideals they once clung to).

7 See Introduction, setting out what we mean by "formalism." See also Stephen G. Nichols, "Modernism and the Politics of Medieval Studies," *Medievalism and the Modernist Temper* 25, 31–32 (R. Howard Bloch & Stephen G. Nichols eds., 1996) (explaining difference between "le dit" and "le dire"—the said and the spoken—and noting how the said "may be taken out of context" so as to support a thesis different from the author's: a standard tool of the formalist lawyer).

8 See chapter 6, *infra*, briefly exploring the medical profession and its recent troubles.

9 Lisa Ruddick, "The Near Enemy of the Humanities Is Professionalism," *Chronicle of Higher Education*, 23 November 2001, § B, p. 7 (lamenting formalism and narrow specialization in the humanities). See also Heidi A. Schuessler, "A Poet Taps into the Disillusionment of Managers," *New York Times*, 20 June 2001, § C, p. 2 (discussing discontent among managers over job uncertainty, longer workdays, shorter vacations, and lack of poetry in their lives); Peter Monaghan, "The 'Insane Little Bubble of Nonreality': That Is Life for Architecture Students," *Chronicle of Higher Education*, 29 June 2001, § A, p. 34 (calling attention to overwork and alienation; students "treated like peons" by teachers who are practicing architects).

10 D. H. Lawrence, *Sons and Lovers* (1913), *Lady Chatterley's Lover* (1928), and "Nottingham and the Mining Countryside," 3 *New Adelphia* (June–August 1930), also in *The Portable D. H. Lawrence* (1977). See also Harry T. Moore, *The Priest of Love: A Life of D. H. Lawrence* (rev. ed. 1974), 29.

11 Might formalism—and its rule of exclusion—be related, as a habit of mind, to the anti-immigrant impulse and nativism (which desire population homogeneity and fear "Balkanization"), English-only initiatives (which aim to achieve a single, canonical language at the expense of linguistic diversity), and support of the Western canon and standardized, Eurocentric school curricula? See generally Bryan Warnick, "Western Culture Is Ugly and Oppressive, and I Am in Its Thrall," *Chronicle of Higher Education*, 15 June 2001, § B, p. 5.

12 For example, the eighty-first case of a will lacking a witness's signature.

13 *Id.*

14 "The Irresponsibles" (1940), 25; see *id.* at 28 ("His pride is to be scientific, neutral, skeptical, detached").

15 See Robert L. Hayman Jr., Nancy Levit, and Richard Delgado, *Jurisprudence, Classical and Contemporary: From Natural Law to Postmodernism* (2d ed. 2002), 156–298. See also Richard Delgado and Jean Stefancic, *Critical Race Theory: An Introduction*, chapter 1 (both setting out this history).

16 See, e.g., his almost rueful praise of Holmes, Frankfurter, and Brandeis in *A Time to Speak: The Selected Prose of Archibald MacLeish* (1941), 166.

17 On these two varieties of formalism, see Jeffrey Malkan, "Literary Formalism, Legal Formalism," 19 *Cardozo Law Review* 1393 (1998).

18 As the movement to secure his release gained force, Pound began reading law, beginning with Blackstone's *Commentaries* and Coke's *Institutes*. He quickly learned that Harvard opened a law department just before the turn of the century and that it was mired in formalism—"some boring buggarin lot of cases and regulations . . . where no principle of law was invoked and NO DEFINITION of terms insisted on . . . there ought to have been atomic destruction of the whole Biddled diddledom." Letter from Ezra Pound to Archibald MacLeish (1 March 1957) (Library of Congress, Manuscript Division, MacLeish File). It took Pound a scant two months to figure out how law school had harmed MacLeish.

19 See chapter 6, *infra* (describing the medical profession and its discontents).

20 See the sections immediately following (on lawyers' complaints), and chapter 5, *infra* (on lawyers' pathologies and disappointments).

21 See sections *infra* on the tribulations of big-firm lawyers, including billable hours, intense competition, and boring, repetitive work.

22 See Andrea Sachs, "Have Law Degree, Will Travel: Fed Up with Thankless Conditions, Many Lawyers Are Taking a Hike," *Time*, 11 December 1999, 106. See also a later section on lawyer burnout and dropout.

23 See Sheila Nielsen, "What Firms Do to Alleviate Attorney Dissatisfaction: Drastic Times Call for Drastic Measures," *Illinois Legal Times*, October 1995, 6.

24 See *id.*; Timothy Harper, "The Best and Brightest, Bored and Burned Out," *A.B.A. Journal*, 15 May 1987, 28.

25 See John Dart, "Public's Esteem of Clergy Slipping: Gallup Poll," *Los Angeles Times*, 2 October 1993, § B, p. 11; Marilyn Kalfus, "Public Perception of Lawyers Declines in Two Opinion Polls," *Orange County Register*, 12 December 1988, § A, p. 1.

26 Dart, *supra* note 25.

27 See Louis Harris, "Changing Trends in American Politics," 510 *Vital Speeches of the Day* 663, 663 (1994) (discussing Harris poll on public trust in various institutions).

28 See Gordon Black, "USA Today Poll," *USA Today*, 20 February 1984.

29 See Barbara Sheehan, "Lawyers Urged to Address Criticisms of Profession,"

New Jersey Law, 26 December 1994, 9; Richard D. Re, "The Causes of Popular Dissatisfaction with the Legal Profession," 68 *St. John's Law Review* 85 (1994).

30 Garry A. Hengstler, "Vox Populi: The Public Perception of Lawyers: ABA Poll," *A.B.A. Journal*, September 1993, 60. See also "Fax Poll," *Lawyer*, March 1992, 96 ("Is Dan Quayle Right?"); Robert Haig, "Lawyer-Bashing: Have We Earned It?," *New York Law Journal*, 19 November 1993, 2 (reporting that 73 percent of Americans think there are too many lawyers).

31 Randall Samborn, "Anti-Lawyer Attitude Up," *National Law Journal*, 9 August 1993, 1.

32 Randall Samborn, "Who's Most Admired Lawyer?," *National Law Journal*, 9 August 1993, 24. The dead lawyers are Thurgood Marshall and Abraham Lincoln. The fictional ones are Perry Mason and Matlock. One of the living lawyers, F. Lee Bailey (the other is Janet Reno), has since been disbarred.

33 See Robert N. Saylor and Anna P. Engh, "Litigators to Examine Lack of Funding, Access," *National Law Journal*, 9 August 1993, § S, p. 3.

34 Catherine Crier, *The Case against Lawyers: How the Lawyers, Politicians, and Bureaucrats Have Turned the Law into an Instrument of Tyranny—and What We as Citizens Have to Do about It* (2002).

35 Daicoff, *supra* note 1, at 1411–13.

36 *Id.*

37 *Id.* at 1413–14.

38 Mona Harrington, *Women Lawyers: Rewriting the Rules* (1994). See also John P. Heinz et al., "Lawyers and Their Discontents," 74 *Indiana Law Journal* 735, 739 (1999); Laurie Albright et al., "Whatever Happened to the Class of 1983?," 78 *Georgetown Law Journal* 153, 163 (1989).

39 "ABA Probes Sources of Lawyer Burnout," *New Jersey Law Journal*, 18 October 1990, 20.

40 "Many Factors Can Lead to Lawyer Burnout," *South Bend Tribune*, 12 March 1995, § A, p. 15 ("Nation/World").

41 Heinz, *supra* note 38, at 739.

42 "The Results from January," *Lawyer*, March 1992, 96 (reporting fax poll).

43 Jill Chanen, "Class of '87: Big Money, Less Satisfaction," *Chicago Lawyer*, October 1993, 1.

44 See a later section, describing conflict between family life and practice in a firm.

45 Heinz, *supra* note 38, at 736.

46 Martha Neil, "Toil Taking Toll, Lawyers Tell Survey," *Chicago Daily Law Bulletin*, 22 August 2000, 1.

47 *Id.*

48 Edward Adams, "Legal Career Exacts Steep Personal Price," *New York Law Journal*, 7 February 1994, 16.

49   *Id.*

50   See Andrea Sachs, *supra* note 22, at 106. On the deadly effect of the billable-hours requirement, see, e.g., Susan Saab Fortney, "Soul for Sale: An Empirical Study of Associate Satisfaction, Law Culture, and the Effects of Billable Hour Requirements," 69 *University of Missouri at Kansas City Law Review* 239 (2000).

51   Deborah L. Arron, "Codependence, Workaholism, and Burnout: A Lawyer's Best Friends?," *Texas Lawyer*, 26 April 1993, 6.

52   Patrick J. Schiltz, "Legal Ethics in Decline: The Elite Law Firm, The Elite Law School, and the Moral Formation of the Novice Attorney," 82 *Minnesota Law Review* 705, 723 (1998).

53   Karen Hall, "Take the Money and Run," *American Lawyer Media*, 16 October 2000.

54   Paul Braverman, "Midlevel Survey," *New York Law Journal*, 13 October 2000, 24.

55   Garance Franke-Ruta, "The Indentured Generation: How Debt Stunts Young People's Dreams," *American Prospect*, summer 2003, § A, p. 22; Robert E. Hirshon, "Graduating under Pressure," *A.B.A. Journal*, November 2001, 6.

56   Adam Liptak, "Stop the Clock? Critics Call the Billable Hour a Legal Fiction," *New York Times*, 29 October 2002, 7 ("On the Job").

57   *Id.*

58   *Id.*

59   *Id.* (quoting Patrick J. Schiltz).

60   *Id.*

61   *Id.*

62   Peter Steinfels, "How Should Time Be Lived? A Professor Sees a Billable-Hours Culture, and Religious Antidotes," *New York Times*, 29 December 2001, § A, p. 10.

63   *Id.*

64   *Id.*

65   "ABA Probes Source of Lawyer Burnout," *supra* note 39, at 20.

66   Chanen, *supra* note 43, at 1.

67   *Id.*

68   "Retention Attention: Top Money Can Be Big Motivator to Leave Firm, but Some Say Churning of Lawyers Is as Much a Byproduct of Employee Dissatisfaction," *Miami Daily Business Review*, 15 June 2001, § A, p. 6. See also the immediately following section (describing how narrow specialization leaves many lawyers bored with their work).

69   See Harper, *supra* note 24, at 28.

70   Michael Orey, "Misery: Legions of Lawyers—Including Partners at Top Firms—Are Unhappy with Their Jobs. What Is the Cause of This Discontent and Is There a Cure?," *American Lawyer*, October 1993, 5.

71 On the rare occasions when an attorney encounters a client, the client will often be angry, frightened, in a rush, or having a dispute about money. "These are the types of situation in which people are generally at their worst—when they lose perspective, behave vindictively, abuse those around them." Mike France, "No: The Hours Are Long. The Stress Is Incredible. And Those Aren't the Worst Parts," *Student Lawyer*, February 1993, 21, 22.

72 Foreword, *Felix Frankfurter, Law and Politics* (1939), xx–xxi.

73 See Archibald MacLeish, "Apologia," 85 *Harvard Law Review* 1505 (1972).

74 See Richard Delgado, "Rodrigo's Thirteenth Chronicle," 95 *Michigan Law Review* 1105, 1116 (1997).

75 "Jumping Ship," *Lawyer*, 5 March 2001, 31.

76 See Alex Johnson, "Think Like a Lawyer, Work Like a Machine: The Dissonance Between Law School and Law Practice," 64 *Southern California Law Review* 1231, 1236–37 (1991).

77 Parick J. Schiltz, "On Being a Happy, Healthy, and Ethical Member of an Unhappy, Unhealthy, and Unethical Profession," 52 *Vanderbilt Law Review* 871, 924–48 (1999); Delgado, *supra* note 74, at 1114; Daphne Eviatar, "Out of Court," *Christian Science Monitor*, 17 April 2000, 11 (on hierarchical nature of many law firms).

78 Schiltz, *supra* note 77; Delgado, *supra* note 74.

79 See Stephen Pepper, "Resisting the Current," 52 *Vanderbilt Law Review* 1015 (1999).

80 See Kathleen E. Hull, "Cross-Examining the Myth of Lawyers' Misery," 52 *Vanderbilt Law Review* 971, 971–72 (1999).

81 Schiltz, *supra* note 77, at 924, 941.

82 Keith Norman, "The Alabama State Bar Quality of Life Survey Results," 55 *Alabama Lawyer* 152, 153 (May 1994).

83 Wendy R. Leibowitz, "The New Fatalism," *American Lawyer*, October 1994, 7.

84 Heinz, *supra* note 38, at 750.

85 Hall, *supra* note 53.

86 Ethan Bronner, "Survey Finds Lawyers Are Generally Happy with Their Careers," *Boston Globe*, 21 May 1990, 3.

87 *Lawyer*, *supra* note 30 (reporting fax poll).

88 Chanen, *supra* note 43.

89 See Adams, *Supro* note 48, at 1.

90 Heinz, *supra* note 38.

91 *Id.*

92 E.g., Fortney, *supra* note 50, at 292–94; Martha Neil, "Brave New World of Partnership," *A.B.A. Journal*, January 2004, 31.

93 Fortney, *supra* note 50; Eviatar, *supra* note 77, at 11; Robert Manor, "New

Competition for Clients, Fees Fuels Growth in Lawyers' Incivility," *Chicago Tribune*, 26 November 2000, § C, p. 1.

94 Manor, *supra* note 93.

95 *Id.*

96 See Adrienne Drell, "Chilling Out: While the Lawyer's Persona of Being Logical and Argumentative May Be the Stuff of Class Comedies—in Real Life These Traits Can Be Anathema to Personal Relationships," *A.B.A. Journal*, October 1994, 70.

97 See Bridget Maloney, "Distress among the Legal Profession: What Law Schools Can Do about It," 15 *Notre Dame Journal of Law, Ethics, and Public Policy* 307, 320 (2001).

98 Manor, *supra* note 93. See also Kronman, *supra* note 6.

99 Manor, *supra* note 93; Norman, *supra* note 82.

100 Manor, *supra* note 93.

101 *Id.*; Terry Carter, "Taking Up the Slack: Law Firms Cut Associates and Costs in the Slowed-Down Economy," *A.B.A. Journal*, October 2001, 22.

102 *Id.*; Patrick J. Schiltz, "Provoking Introspection: A Reply to Galanter & Palay, Hull, Kelly, Lesnick, McLaughlin, Pepper, and Traynor," 52 *Vanderbilt Law Review* 1033, 1044–50 (1999).

103 Carter, *supra* note 101.

104 Schiltz, *supra* note 77, at 1017.

105 See Hengstler, *supra* note 30.

106 See Fortney, *supra* note 50.

107 Schiltz, *supra* note 52, at 740.

108 *Id.* See also Manor, *supra* note 93; Norman, *supra* note 82, at 153–56.

109 Schiltz, *supra* note 52, at 740–47.

110 "Lawyers Looking at You," *Fortune*, January 1931, 61, 61.

111 Norman, *supra* note 82, at 153.

112 *Id.* at 156.

113 Fortney, *supra* note 50, at 289.

114 *Id.* at 290–91.

115 Mark Hansen, "A Shunned Justice System: Most Families Don't Turn to Lawyers or Judges to Solve Legal Problems," *A.B.A. Journal*, April 1994, 18.

116 *Id.*

117 See *supra* notes 17–31 and accompanying text, this chapter.

118 See *supra* notes 23–25 and accompanying text, this chapter; Daicoff, *supra* note 1, at 543, 552.

119 See Norman, *supra* note 82, at 153.

120 *Id.*

121 Mike France, "Can Law Practice Be Fun?," *Student Lawyer*, February 1993, 20–21.

122 See Harper, *supra* note 24; Albright et al., *supra* note 38.

123 Albright et al., *supra* note 38.

124 See Nancy D. Holt, "Are Longer Hours Here to Stay? Quality Time Losing Out," *A.B.A. Journal*, February 1993, 62.

125 *Id.*

126 *Id.* at 64.

127 James S. Granelli, "The Happiest Lawyers: They Teach," *National Law Journal*, 11 August 1989, 10.

5 Lawyers' Lives

1 For a vivid account, see Scott Turow, *One L* (1977). See also Seth Stern, "Harvard Changes the Pace of Its Paper Chase," *Christian Science Monitor*, 24 October 2000; Bridget A. Maloney, "Distress among the Legal Profession: What Law Schools Can Do about It," 15 *Notre Dame Journal of Law, Ethics, and Public Policy* 307, 324–25 (2001).

2 See Lani Guinier et al., "Becoming Gentlemen: Women's Experiences at One Ivy League Law School," 143 *University of Pennsylvania Law Review* 1 (1994).

3 Stern, *supra* note 1.

4 *Id.*

5 Lawrence S. Krieger, "Institutional Denial about the Dark Side of Law School, and Fresh Empirical Guidance for Constructively Breaking the Silence," 52 *Journal of Legal Education* 111 (2002).

6 See Susan Daicoff, "Asking Leopards to Change Their Spots: Should Lawyers Change? A Critique of Solutions to Problems with Professionalism by Reference to Empirically Derived Attorney Personality Attributes," 11 *Georgetown Journal of Legal Ethics* 547 (1998).

7 Lawrence S. Krieger, "What We're Not Telling Law Students and Lawyers That They Really Need to Know: Some Thoughts-in-Action toward Revitalizing the Profession from Its Roots," 13 *Journal of Law and Health* 1 (1998).

8 See Alex Johnson, "Think Like a Lawyer, Work Like a Machine: The Dissonance between Law School and Law Practice," 64 *Southern California Law Review* 1231 (1991).

9 See chapter 4, *supra*, and the immediately following sections to see some remarkable parallels. See also Anne Fahy Morris, " 'Justifiable Paranoia' Afflicts Lawyers, Psychologist Says; Stress: He Tries to Teach Attorneys How to Deal

with Problems They Face, Including Public Revulsion, Depression, Divorce, Alcoholism, Drug Addiction," *Los Angeles Times*, 1 May 1994, 27; Maloney, *supra* note 1.

10   See David R. Culp, "Law School: A Mortuary for Poets and Moral Reason," 16 *Campbell Law Review* 61 (1994).

11   *Id.*

12   *Id.* at 93 (quoting Kafka, "Dear Father"). See also *id.* at 61–86, positing that the Socratic method, stress, and competition shut down creativity and open a split between the emotions and the rational processes. Might the production of cool, dispassionate professionals ready to do the various kinds of antisocial work that big corporations need done be the very point of legal education conducted in this fashion?

13   Andrea Wang (private communication, 14 March 2001).

14   Daicoff, *supra* note 6, at 547.

15   See chapter 4, *supra*, at note 78 and accompanying text (reporting on lawyers' belief that civility is declining throughout the profession). See also Robert Manor, "New Competition for Clients, Fees Fuels Growth in Lawyers' Incivility," *Chicago Tribune*, 26 November 2000, § C, p. 1; Daicoff, *supra* note 6, at 547–48.

16   Daicoff, *supra* note 6, at 553.

17   See Ed Honnold, "Tackling the Source of Career Malaise Can Be Hard Work," *Legal Times*, 17 May 1992, § S, p. 28.

18   *Id.*

19   *Id.*

20   Daphne Eviatar, "Out of Court," *Christian Science Monitor*, 17 April 2000, 11.

21   See Susan Saab Fortney, "Soul for Sale: An Empirical Study of Associate Satisfaction, Law Firm Culture, and the Effects of Billable Hour Requirements," 69 *University of Missouri at Kansas City Law Review* 239, 264 (2000).

22   *Id.*

23   *Id.*

24   *Id.*

25   *Id.* at 265.

26   *Id.*

27   *Id.* at 266.

28   *Id.*

29   *Id.*

30   Honnold, *supra* note 17.

31   *Id.*

32   Fortney, *supra* note 21, at 270.

33 *Id.* at 271.

34 *Id.*

35 See *id.* at 273.

36 See Patrick J. Schiltz, "On Being a Happy, Healthy, and Ethical Member of an Unhappy, Unhealthy, and Unethical Profession," 52 *Vanderbilt Law Review* 871, 880–81 (1999).

37 *Id.*

38 "Report of the AALS Special Committee on Problems of Substance Abuse in The Law Schools," 44 *Journal of Legal Education* 42–44 (1994).

39 *Id.* at 41–45.

40 *Id.* at 45–50.

41 See Dale Adams, "Alcohol, Drugs, and Law Practice: Representing the Chemically Dependent Attorney," 76 *Michigan Bar Journal* 294 (1997).

42 Gerald W. Boston, "Chemical Dependency in Legal Education: Problems and Strategies," 76 *Michigan Bar Journal* 298, 298–300 (1997); Schiltz, *supra* note 36, at 877–78.

43 Scott Donaldson, *Archibald MacLeish: An American Life* (1992), 419, 430, 473; William MacLeish, *Uphill with Archie* (2001), 203.

44 Schiltz, *supra* note 36, at 877.

45 *Id.* at 877–78.

46 Daicoff, *supra* note 6, at 555.

47 Schiltz, *supra* note 36, at 876.

48 See Connie Beck et al., "Lawyer Distress," 19 *Journal of Law and Health* 1, 3 (1995).

49 See Morris, *supra* note 9, at 27.

50 See, e.g., George Edward Bailey, "Impairment, The Profession, and Your Law Partner," 15 *Maine Bar Journal* 96 (2000); Tricia S. Heil, "From Gatekeeping to Disbarment and Back Again: Chemical Dependency and Mental Health Issues in Licensing and Discipline," 64 *Texas Bar Journal* 158 (2001); William John Kane and Cheryl Baisden, "Use and Abuse: Are You Controlling the Substance or Is the Substance Controlling You?," *New Jersey Lawyer*, December 1996, 12.

51 E.g., Bailey, *supra* note 50; Heil, *supra* note 50.

52 Jennifer L. Reichert, "Lawyers and Substance Abuse," *Trial*, 1 June 2000, 76.

53 See Connie Beck et al., "Lawyer Distress: Alcohol-Related Problems and Other Psychological Concerns among a Sample of Practicing Lawyers," 10 *Journal of Law and Health* 1, 6–9 (1996).

54 *Id.*

55 *Id.*

56 *Id.* at 8.

57 See Terry Carter, "Your Time or Your Money: Groundswell Supports Less Bill-able Hours, Alternate Tracks to the Top," *A.B.A. Journal*, February 2001, 26.

58 Schiltz, *supra* note 36, at 878.

59 *Id.*

60 *Id.*

61 See Adrienne Drell, "Chilling Out: While the Lawyer's Persona of Being Logical and Argumentative May Be the Stuff of Class Comedies—in Real Life These Traits Can Be Anathema to Personal Relationships," *A.B.A. Journal*, October 1994, 70.

62 See Donaldson, *supra* note 43, at 141, 190–91, 473–76. See also *id.* at 389 (reporting that he opposed his daughter's marriage to a Navy ensign because of his lower-class origins); *Uphill with Archie*, *supra* note 43, at 76–78 (reporting that MacLeish was a detached father).

63 See Kane and Baisden, *supra* note 50, at 12.

64 *Id.* at 12.

65 See Schiltz, *supra* note 36, at 874.

66 *Id.*

67 *Id.* at 874.

68 *Id.*

69 Andrea Sachs, "First, Kiss All the Lawyers: Can the Legal Profession Salvage Its Image from an Onslaught of Lawyer Bashing?," *Time*, 16 August 1993, 39.

70 Schiltz, *supra* note 36, at 880.

71 *Id.*

72 *Id.* at 881.

73 The article was Timothy Harper, "The Best and Brightest, Bored and Drop-ping Out," 73 *A.B.A. Journal*, May 1987, 28.

74 *Id.* at 28.

75 *Id.*

76 *Id.*

77 *Id.*

78 Schiltz, *supra* note 36, at 882.

79 *Id.* at 882–83.

80 Mike France, "Can Law Practice Be Fun?," *Student Lawyer*, February 1993, 20.

81 *Id.* at 884.

82 See Young Lawyers Division, American Bar Association, *Career Satisfaction 1995*, n. 1 (1995).

83 See Eviatar, *supra* note 20, at 11.

84 Scott Barancik, "Lawyers Who Leave," *St. Petersburg Times*, 3 July 2000, § E, p. 8.

85 *Id.*

86 France, *supra* note 80.

87 Eviatar, *supra* note 20.

88 Harper, *supra* note 73.

89 Barancik, *supra* note 84.

90 See chapter 4, *supra*, at note 65 and accompanying text.

91 See *id.* at text and notes 68–69, 72, 77. See also chapter 3, *supra*, at notes 22–23 and accompanying text.

92 See *id.* at note 83 and accompanying text.

93 See note 24, this chapter, and accompanying text.

94 See chapter 4, *supra*, at notes 80 and 122 and accompanying text.

95 See Deborah Rhode, "Pro Bono in Principle and in Practice," 53 *Journal of Legal Education* 413 (2003); Laura Gatland, "Dangerous Dedication," *A.B.A. Journal* 28 (December 1997).

96 See chapter 4, *supra*, at note 123 and accompanying text.

97 See, e.g., James M. Doyle, " 'It's the Third World Down There!': The Colonialist Vocation and American Criminal Justice," 27 *Harvard Civil Rights–Civil Liberties Law Review* 71 (1992).

6 Other Professions

1 But see Sally Satel, PC, M.D., *How Political Correctness Is Corrupting Medicine* (2001) (urging that the problem with medicine is not corporatization or dehumanizing managed care, but feminism and touchy-feely, left-wing social thought that makes victims of the poor and of overworked interns). See also chapter 4, *supra*, at note 7 and accompanying text (listing other professions suffering from regimentation of thought or work).

2 See "Physicians Reach All-Time High in Discontent with Managed Care," 63 *Health Industry Today*, 1 August 2000; Michael Perrault, "Code Blue for M.D.s: Doctors Burn Out under Burden of Red Tape, Loss of Independence," *Rocky Mountain News*, 7 April 2001, § C, p. 1.

3 "Physicians Reach All-Time High in Discontent," *supra* note 2; Perrault, *supra* note 2; "Doctors Still Unhappy with HMO Plans," AP Newswire, 30 June 2000.

4 "Physicians Reach All-Time High in Discontent," *supra* note 2.

5 See Mohammedreza Hojat et al., "Physicians' Perceptions of the Changing Healthcare System," 25 *Journal of Community Health*, 1 December 2000.

6 "Doctors' Discontent Is a Troubling Symptom," *Washington Post*, 6 February 2001 (quoting the internist Edward Campion).

7 See Rebecca Lentz, "They've Had Enough," *Modern Physician*, 1 August 2000,

12; Dorothy Bonn, "Work-Related Stress: Can It Be a Thing of the Past?," *Lancet*, 8 January 2000, 124 (noting that doctors in the United States complain widely about losing autonomy because of managed care).

8 Lentz, *supra* note 7.

9 Liz Kowalczyk, "More Doctors Unhappy with Managed Care," *Boston Globe*, 30 June 2000.

10 Luci Asommer et al., "A Descriptive Study of Managed Care Hassles in 26 Practices," *Western Journal of Medicine*, 1 March 2001, 174.

11 Bryan P. Bergeron, "Where to Find Practical Patient Education Materials," 106 *Digital Doctor*, November 1999, 35.

12 Julie Marquis, "Doctors Who Lose Patience," *Los Angeles Times*, 3 March 1999, § A, p. 1.

13 Julie Karsh, "Burned-Out Doctors Increasingly Seek Other Lines of Work," *Kansas City Star*, 22 January 2001.

14 *Id.*

15 *Id.*

16 Carl T. Hall, "Younger Doctors Disheartened: Many Complain of Intrusion of the Bottom Line," *San Francisco Chronicle*, 18 November 1995, § B, p. 1 ("Business").

17 Thomas H. Gallagher, "Patients' Attitudes toward Cost Control Bonuses for Managed Care Physicians," *Health Affairs*, March–April 2001.

18 John G. Hope, "Physician, Heal Thyself," *Modern Physician*, 1 April 2000, 88.

19 Dorothy Bonn and John Bonn, "Work-Related Stress," *Lancet*, 8 January 2000, 124.

20 A. J. Ramirez et al., "Mental Health of Hospital Consultants: The Effects of Stress and Satisfaction at Work," *Lancet*, 16 March 1996, 724; Donald K. Freeborn et al., "Satisfaction, Commitment, and Psychological Well-being Among HMO Physicians," *Western Journal of Medicine*, 1 January 2001, 1.

21 Eric Williams et al., "Understanding Physicians' Intention to Leave Practice," *Health Care Management Review*, 1 January 2001, 719.

22 Hope, *supra* note 18.

23 American Medical Association, "Substance Abuse among Physicians," Report no. 1, Council of Scientific Affairs, A-95 (but finding that physicians use more alcohol and abuse prescription drugs, including opiates, more than the population at large).

24 See "Scope-of-Care: Primary Care Doctors Feel Pressure," *American Health Line*, 23 December 1999 (doctors dissatisfied with gate-keeping function of managed care medicine).

25 Margaret Ann Cross, "Slicing It Thin," *Modern Physician*, 1 November 1999, 56.

26 Avedis Donabedian, "An Expert on Health Care Evaluates His Own Case," *New York Times*, 12 June 2001, § D, p. 6.

27 See Liana R. Clark, "How Do We Get Back Our Humanity?," *Medical Economics*, 7 May 2001, 96; Joseph Herman, "The Good Old Days," *Lancet*, 12 December 1998, 1930; Kelly Crow, "Healing and Burnout, 12 Hours at a Stretch," *New York Times*, 24 June 2001, § 15, p. 2 (on stress and burnout among nurses).

28 Clark, *supra* note 27, at 96.

29 *Id.*

30 Roger Higgs et al., "Changing Face of Medical Curricula," *Lancet*, 3 March 2001, 357.

31 Dinitia Smith, "Diagnosis Goes Low Tech," *New York Times*, 11 October 2003, § B, p. 9.

32 Howard Markel, "Doctors Now Need Well Honed Skills in Job Hunting," *New York Times*, 22 May 2001, § F, p. 5.

33 Hall, *supra* note 16.

34 *Id.*

35 Anna Navarro, "Physician Brain Drain Emerges as Docs Drop Medicine," *St. Louis Business Journal*, 7 August 2000, 20. See also Matt Richtel, "Young Doctors and Wish Lists: No Weekend Calls, No Beepers," *New York Times*, 7 January 2004, § A, p. 1 (doctors shifting to specialties like dermatology which offer more humane working conditions).

36 Marquis, *supra* note 12, at § A, p. 1; Bonn, *supra* note 7.

37 Marquis, *supra* note 12.

38 Lentz, *supra* note 7, at 12.

39 Perrault, *supra* note 2; Devin Friedman, "Dr. Levine's Dilemma," *New York Times Magazine*, 5 May 2002, 66.

40 Marquis, *supra* note 12.

41 "Medical Schools: Application Numbers Falling," *American Health Line*, 2 November 1992; Diana Jean Schemo, "Medical School Applications Dip Sharply; Minorities' Rise Slightly," *New York Times*, 27 October 2000, § A, p. 18.

42 Lentz, *supra* note 7.

43 Neil Chesanow, "Would You Want Your Kids to Follow in Your Footsteps?," *Medical Economics*, 10 January 2000, 98.

44 Hall, *supra* note 16.

7 High-Paid Misery

1 See chapter 4, *supra*, at notes 1–2.

2 See Patrick J. Schiltz, "Legal Ethics in Decline: The Elite Law Firm, the Elite

Law School, and the Moral Formation of the Novice Attorney," 82 *Minnesota Law Review* 705, 739 (1998); David R. Edelstein, "A Challenge to Your Mental Health," *Chicago Bar Record* 24, 24 (1994).

3 See Duncan Kennedy, "Legal Education and the Reproduction of Hierarchy," 32 *Journal of Legal Education* 591 (1982) (analyzing political aspects of legal education and practice).

4 See Mona Harrington, *Women Lawyers: Rewriting the Rules* (1994) (urging restructuring of legal culture, especially the large-firm variety); Kathryn Abrams, "Gender, Discrimination, and the Transformation of Workplace Norms," 42 *Vanderbilt Law Review* 1183, 1184–85 (1989); Terry Carter, "Your Time or Your Money: Groundswell Supports Less Billable Hours, Alternate Tracks to the Top," *A.B.A. Journal*, February 2001, 26; Marci A. Nusbaum, "Flex in Flux, Alternative Work Options Go beyond the 'Mommy Track,' " *Life* (Liberty Law School), summer 2001, 16.

5 Marci Alboher Nusbaum, "Closing His Eyes, He Sees a Path," *New York Times*, 28 September 2003, 2 ("Business"); "Many Factors Can Lead to Lawyer Burnout," *South Bend Tribune*, 12 March 1995, § A, p. 15 (reporting that New York State Bar Association recently published a Handbook on Stress Management for Lawyers). See also Steven Keeva, "Transforming Practices: Finding Joy and Satisfaction in the Legal Life" (American Bar Association, 1996); Ann L. Iijima, "Lessons Learned: Legal Education and Law Student Dysfunction," 48 *Journal of Legal Education* 524, 529 (December 1998) (suggesting physical exercise).

6 See, e.g., Janet Weinstein, "Coming of Age: Recognizing the Importance of Interdisciplinary Education in Law Practice," 74 *Washington Law Review* 319 (1999) (advocating interdisciplinary perspectives); C. M. A. McCauliff and Paula A. Franzese, "Mother Teresa's Legacy to Lawyers," 28 *Seton Hall Law Review* 765 (1998) (urging attention to public-service and spiritual dimensions of law practice); Kennedy, *supra* note 3. See also Scott Hunter, "Tapping Our Intrinsic Motivation," *Connecticut Law Tribune*, 16 September 1996 (urging restructuring of law practice to facilitate lawyers' creativity and access to meaningful work, and to acknowledge and appreciate their contribution); Jamison Wilcox, "Borrowing Experience: Using Reflective Lawyer Narratives in Teaching," 50 *Journal of Legal Education* 213 (2000) (urging that students read accounts of successful activist lawyers, because "The old saw is that the law sharpens the mind by narrowing it. In fact, travels in the law can be as broadening as any. But legal education does narrow the mind in certain ways. . . . Legal education studies texts that are severely limited, and it tries to banish as irrelevant many of the thoughts and feelings that students bring to the stories they encounter in those texts or elsewhere").

7 See, e.g., Thomas C. Grey, *The Wallace Stevens Case: Law and the Practice of Poetry* (2001) (pointing out that Stevens seemed capable of compartmentalizing his boring insurance-law practice and his life as a poet so that what he did for a living did not kill off his poetry).

　　Might MacLeish, as a young writer, have been struggling with just these issues? After a visit to the older lawyer-poet, Stevens, in 1925, MacLeish wrote to him of their conversation: "You can write the waste of time off to charity . . . it meant a great deal to me." See Scott Donaldson, *Archibald MacLeish: An American Life* (1992), 153.

8 See Richard A. Posner, "Legal Formalism, Legal Realism, and the Interpretations of Statutes and the Constitution," 37 *Case Western Reserve Law Review* 179, 184 (1987) ("The modern exemplar of formalism in common law is the positive economic analysis of that law which Professor Landes and I and others have expounded. Taking as our premise the claim that the common law seeks to promote efficiency in the sense of wealth maximization . . . we deduce a set of optimal common law doctrines and institutions and then compare them with the actual common law").

9 See, e.g., Carol Andreas, *Meatpackers and Beef Barons: Company Town in a Global Economy* (1994).

10 See Archibald MacLeish, "Modern Instances: Notebooks, 1924–1938," 73 *Poetry* 33 (October 1948–March 1949) ("It is not the poet's part to impose order by fiat like a ruler, or by argument like a philosopher, or by faith like a saint, but to discover it. If it exists and where it exists and not otherwise. Even though he finds it in its opposite as Empedocles did who said that the universe exists by virtue of the discord of its elements and that if harmony were to take the place of discord the universe would disrupt into chaos").

11 Mark Warren Bailey, "Early Legal Education in the United States: Natural Law Theory and Law as a Moral Science," 48 *Journal of Legal Education* 311 (1998).

Index

JEAN STEFANCIC is a research professor
of law and the Derrick Bell Scholar in
Law at the University of Pittsburgh
School of Law.

RICHARD DELGADO is a professor of law
and the Derrick Bell Fellow in Law at
the University of Pittsburgh School
of Law.